NETWORK MARKETING FOR INTROVERTS:
A GUIDE FOR THE SHY, TIMID AND RESERVED

Jenifer Kay Hood

©2014

The 16 Myers-Briggs Types			
http://www.myersbriggs.org/			
US Population Breakdown			
The table organizing the sixteen types was created by Isabel Myers (an INFP person).			
ISTJ	ISFJ	INFJ	INTJ
11–14%	9–14%	1–3%	2–4%
ISTP	ISFP	INFP	INTP
4–6%	5–9%	4–5%	3–5%
ESTP	ESFP	ENFP	ENTP
4–5%	4–9%	6–8%	2–5%
ESTJ	ESFJ	ENFJ	ENTJ
8–12%	9–13%	2–5%	2–5%
Estimated percentages of the 16 types in the U.S. population.[29]			

"Originality thrives in seclusion free of outside influences beating upon us to cripple the creative mind. Be alone — that is the secret of invention: be alone, that is when ideas are born." ~ Nikola Tesla

Table of Contents

Chapter 1: Lost Opportunity 4

Chapter 2: How and Why I Got Started in Network Marketing ... 7

Chapter 3: Why There is a Need for This Book 11

Chapter 4: Nurturing Your Authentic Self 17

Chapter 5: Preparing Your Mind and Heart 25

Chapter 6: Preparing To Go Into Business 34

Chapter 7: Communication Matters 40

Chapter 8: Making A List, Checking It Twice 57

Chapter 9: Going From Wallflower to Social Butterfly 62

Chapter 10: Doable Dozen for Network Marketing Success 70

Chapter 11: Using Social Media 76

Chapter 12: Use Your Tools 84

Chapter 13: Supporting Your Introverted Downlines 89

Chapter 14: Nurturing Your Future 106

Chapter 15: Great Reads To Help You In the Process 120

Acknowledgments 122

Chapter 1. Lost Opportunity

"The value of an idea lies in the using of it." ~ *Thomas Edison*

Let's face it: network marketing is a people business. Extroverts are naturals in the field because they get their energy from reaching out. Plus, they often have a large social network. Meanwhile, introverts are discouraged from this multibillion dollar industry because their energy comes from within and they often have a relatively small group of intimate friends and family.

I get it. I know why the extroverts in network marketing keep insisting introverts model their behavior. They want us to have more contacts. But they want us to get them on their terms, by their rules. We introverts take years to build our networks and rely on a close knit circle of supporters. We cherish our little band of eight to ten friends. Which is why we resist the extroverted model. It just feels impossible.

It isn't that introverts don't know how to make friends. In fact, many introverts can serve in very public ways, making speeches or otherwise appearing to be extroverts. Yet the introvert's authentic self remains reserved, self-contained, thoughtful, and often shy.

Consequently, we tend to think of ourselves as poorly suited to network marketing and so allow an exceptionally rewarding opportunity to pass us by. We tell ourselves that we are not suited to the field because we would rather be alone than network. We even try to discourage our involvement in the model because we believe it must be some kind of scam perpetrated on less intelligent folks by the people at the top of a pyramid. Consequently, we self-select lost opportunity.

Furthermore, many extroverted "uplines" (meaning the people who recruited us) tell us we'll never make it. They discourage us from finding our own way and insist the business can only be done their way. They tell us we're:

- Lazy
- Stubborn
- Unteachable/Uncoachable
- Arrogant
- Incapable
- Making excuses

But are we really? Why should we be labeled negatively just because as introverts we approach life differently? Maybe the actual truth is that we have the following traits of a *master* network marketer:

- Thoughtful
- Good Listener
- Trustworthy
- Persistent
- Creative
- Passionate

And if this is true, think of the difference a company could make if it didn't lose half its sales staff every few months because network marketing "wasn't for them." Consider the impact it would have on a company if they took advantage of the introvert's many gifts!

For example, testing by psychologist Gerald Matthews indicates, "Introverts think before they act, digest information thoroughly, stay on task longer, give up less easily, and work more accurately."[1] Sounds like a recipe for network marketing success! So why isn't someone teaching us how to get past our supposed limitations and embrace our authentic self so we too can succeed in this billion dollar industry?

Well, you're in luck.

This book will help you break that paradigm. You will learn tried and true techniques for building a customer base, keeping friendships, honoring family, and putting principles before profits. From this day forward you'll know what it takes to be an introverted network marketing professional. You'll learn how to build your team, be more at ease socially, broaden your sphere, use social media, and employ your natural gifts to stay in the flow of consistent performance, while our extroverted peers will learn how to support introverted down lines and keep them in the game.

---

[1] Cain, Susan. *Quiet: The Power of Introverts in a World That Can't Stop Talking*, New York: Broadway Books. 2013. 168.

Chapter 2. How and Why I Got Started in Network Marketing

> *"I am a horse for a single harness, not cut out for tandem or teamwork; for well I know that in order to attain any definite goal, it is imperative that one person do the thinking and the commanding."*
> ~ *Albert Einstein*

As an introvert I know how important it is to be my authentic self. A side benefit of this character trait is that I have excellent radar about the trueness of others. When a friend approached me about network marketing, she didn't know I had already turned down at least ten opportunities to participate in this driver of a new economy. People assumed I must be super outgoing because I was able to make speeches and be the economic development face of a community. Nothing could have been further from the truth. I was — and am — an introvert.

In November 2012, I realized my job was about to end. I meditate daily and keep a journal of my thoughts. As the winter's chill blew dead leaves against my house, I began to pray.

I got it! I needed to identify the perfect job, so I described the perfect position, one that was, "stable, effective, safe, fun, rewarding, sustainable, remarkable, inspiring, respectful, collegial, satisfying, relaxed, well-paid and influential." Eight months later in July 2013, I was still stuck in the same miserable job, but by that time I'd been given notice. My job would be over at the end of the month.

That's when my friend Karen offered her company as a solution. I immediately got my hackles up. "No, damn it," I thought, "not another person who thinks I can be their down line money maker in some pyramid scheme." Yet I knew Karen was a sincere and loving person, so I decided to hear her out. After all, I suspected Karen was also at least partially introverted. Surely she would understand when I explained why I didn't have what it takes to succeed in a people business. Fully ready to tell her, "No, thank you," I let her acquaint me with her product.

Why? Because back in December 2012, two weeks after I'd asked God to guide me to a perfect job, a drawing of the product Karen sold came to me in meditation. I had no idea what Karen did for a living. When I met her a year earlier, she had told me she was a waitress, so I figured that's what she still did. She had never approached me about her product, so I was surprised when she described it. It was just as I had drawn in my journal two weeks after praying for the perfect job!

The graphic I'd drawn was accompanied by a phrase that indicated this was the answer to my prayer. But at the time I couldn't figure out what the product was. Google was no help. Yet when Karen described the product, I immediately remembered the drawing and knew this lead was heaven sent.

Add to this the remarkable results I got when I tried the product. As much as I trust God, I knew I couldn't promote any product I didn't believe in. How could I belong to something unless it reflected the person I hoped to become? So I started using the product on July 26, 2013; by August 5, 2013, I was already noticing the dramatic healing effects of my product. My bladder control issue was rapidly improving. My skin had a fresh glow. I was sleeping better and had more energy than I'd had in years — and all this after coming off a miserable job that had depleted my drive.

That's when I became an associate with my company.

A month later, my bladder issue was gone, age spots were fading, and the dark circles under my eyes were greatly diminished. A month after that, my hearing and eyesight had noticeably improved. My jowls were going away as my skin began to get firmer. By December 2013, the color was returning to my lips and my thinning eyebrows no longer needed pencil to look fully visible. Consequently, I was ready to really take network marketing seriously and devote myself to it full time in January 2014. My devotion to my business grew even stronger when, in April 2014, I noticed my joint pain was greatly reduced, my fingernails were tougher than they had ever been, and a lifelong issue with depth perception (caused by my eyes not working together) had begun to correct itself.

In short, I found the right company and the right product. I began to build a team. I found myself doing things I never thought I would do. I created a model that took the best of what the most successful network marketers were doing and combined it with what I, as an introvert, could comfortably do.

Why should I self-select the potential loss of millions just because I wasn't prom queen? I could be the belle of the ball — even if that ball was a little quieter and a bit more cerebral than the average Saturday night dance.

Chapter 3. Why There Is a Need for This Book

"Whatever kind of introvert you are, some people will find you "too much" in some ways and "not enough" in others." ~ Laurie Helgoe

As much as I like my company, our product, and working with my centroverted friend Karen, everything was not sunshine and roses. It was still network marketing and required all the things which that business normally asks of its associates.

I knew experts agreed that most people employ at least some elements of both introversion and extroversion in their daily lives, but they also acknowledge there is usually a more dominant side of the personality equation. According to educators Jill D. Burruss and Lisa Kaenzig, this is "especially [true] in times of stress."[2]

This observation fit me to a tee. For example, when I went to my first convention in September 2013, I felt completely overwhelmed. The only person I had any knowledge of was Karen, but I hardly knew her and she was completely swept up in the convention hoopla. All I heard was "rah, rah, rah," and, "you just have to get used to the idea of cornering all your friends and speaking to anyone within three feet of you." I despaired. Really, God, do I have to tackle people in grocery stores?

---

[2] Burris, Jill and Kaenzig, Lisa. *Virginia Association for the Gifted Newsletter.* 1999, Fall. 21.

I spoke with Karen about it. As my upline, I hoped she could guide me to get beyond my introversion. I figured since she was already moving up the associate ladder, she must have found a method that worked for her introverted side. But she offered me the same techniques everyone else had. Discouraged, but still convinced God had put me in front of this product for a reason, I began to explore strategies to help people like me work this business. I knew if I couldn't find a solution, my business, and the company I had chosen to work with, would lose associates at the same rate every network marketing company does. The statistics[3] are staggering:

- In the first year of operation, a minimum of 50% of representatives drop out.
- After five years of operation, a minimum of 90% of representatives have left the company.
- By year 10, only those at or near the top have not dropped out – making it safe to say at least 95% of representatives have dropped out.

The researcher, Dr. Jon M. Taylor, theorized that people were quitting network marketing because they weren't making any money. However, if one looks at the statistics under the lens of introvert/extrovert percentages, it is likely the majority of the 50% first year loss may largely reflect the 50% of people who are introverts. Extrapolating from there, one can see percentages might increase as the number of introverts are recruited. This doesn't mean extroverts never

---

[3] http://homebusiness.about.com/od/homebusinessprofiles/a/The-Likelihood-Of-Mlm-Success.htm

fail or drop out. There are probably other reasons for that happening. Yet I believe if introverts could find a way to successfully overcome their genetic predisposition against the "three feet rule" (the practice of trying to connect to anyone within three feet of you), the dropout rate would be significantly lower.

This is why I began to think of ways I could be a success in this business. I already knew that introverts approach the world differently, but I wanted to find a way to articulate those differences. That is when I found this explanation:

> "The extravert's flow is directed outward toward people and objects, and the introvert's is directed inward toward concepts and ideas. Contrasting characteristics between extraverts and introverts include the following:
>
> - Extraverts are "action" oriented, while introverts are "thought" oriented.
> - Extraverts seek "breadth" of knowledge and influence, while introverts seek "depth" of knowledge and influence.
> - Extraverts often prefer more "frequent" interaction, while introverts prefer more "substantial" interaction.
> - Extraverts recharge and get their energy from spending time with people, while introverts recharge and get their energy from spending time

alone; they consume their energy through the opposite process."[4]

In short, extroverts are influenced by people; introverts are influenced by facts. Thus in order to be a success in network marketing, I would need enough confidence in what I was saying to present my position as a verifiable fact and find ways to be out there enough to build a team, while still giving myself time to recharge privately.

The solution!

I started to research ways I could negotiate around my quiet authentic self and cultivate skills to help me make enough contacts in this people-oriented business. I began with reading works by Susan Cain, Laurie Helgoe, and Deborah Zach, introverts who have been hugely successful in the consulting field. I studied the Meyers-Briggs personality test, and learned why I respond the way I do certain stimuli. By the way, during that process, I discovered that Isabel Briggs Meyers was an INFP (introverted, intuitive, feeling, and perceiving) type...just like me.

---

[4]Paul D. Tieger and Barbara Barron-Tieger. *The Art of Speed Reading People*, 1999. New York, NY: Little, Brown and Company, 66.

But I didn't just gain from learning more about introversion. I also looked into what successful extroverted network marketers were doing. I dug deep into Eric Worre's *Go Pro*, and paid attention to Steve Shapiro's *Listening for Success*. I even took into account what extroverts like Jim Rohn, Zig Ziglar, and Stephen Covey had to say about the industry. Finally, I looked at the number of multi-millionaires who believe network marketing is the future of business in America. If millionaires like Donald Trump, Robert Kiyosaki and Warren Buffet see value in the model, who am I to question its validity?

I shared the ideas of these experts and my own instinctive techniques with higher-ups. Instead of telling me, "No," they applauded my attempt to find a solution, yet warned me that people had been trying to find their own way of doing this business for years without success. I was pleased when trainings started offering ideas for introverts to try, but the emphasis was still on the "Three Feet Rule." I knew I would never be able to approach everyone within three feet of me, so I started to generate and test some techniques that would work for introverts like myself. Without an alternative to traditional techniques, introverts, centroverts, and even many extroverts would fail completely. Given my penchant for wanting to help others — not to mention my growing belief in the model — I decided to test my theories and, if they worked, pass them along.

How to use this book

Throughout this book you will find highlighted boxes labeled, "Today's Network Marketing Tip." At a glance you will be able to get the core of that chapter's lesson or lessons. Read these carefully. They are densely packed nuggets to help make more effective use of your time and reduce discouragement.

You will benefit from reading this book cover to cover, as well as the various works listed in the bibliography. As you go along, make notes of the areas where you're having trouble, and feel free to visit my Facebook page, "Network Marketing for Introverts," to drop me a line or ask a question. I will try to answer promptly.

You can be a success in this business! You already have the necessary tools. Keep going! Don't give up. Before you know it you'll be managing a large, prosperous, and professional network marketing business.

Chapter 4. Honouring Your Authentic Self

"Success is liking yourself, liking what you do, and liking how you do it." ~ *Maya Angelou*

As an introvert, you approach the world differently than an extrovert. If you try to be something you're not, you will find yourself depressed, confused or, even worse for would-be network marketers, pushy to the point of being obnoxious. Yet you are constantly confronted by leaders in the field who give the impression that you are somehow lacking and have to change.

I believe Jonathan Rausch sums the plight of the introvert extremely well in an article in the March 2003 *Atlantic Monthly:*

In our extrovertist society, being outgoing is considered normal and therefore desirable, a mark of happiness, confidence, leadership. Extroverts are seen as bighearted, vibrant, warm, empathic. 'People person' is a compliment. Introverts are described with words like 'guarded,' 'loner,' 'reserved,' 'taciturn,' 'self-contained,' 'private' — narrow, ungenerous words, words that suggest emotional parsimony and smallness of personality. Female introverts,

I suspect, must suffer especially. In certain circles, particularly in the Midwest, a man can still sometimes get away with being what they used to call a strong and silent type; introverted women, lacking that alternative, are even more likely than men to be perceived as timid, withdrawn, haughty.

Portrait of an Introvert

Now that we know how the extrovert world sees us, let's start dispelling some of those myths by identifying some characteristics your authentic introverted self would identify with[5]:

- If given the right space, you can concentrate well and deeply.
- You often become absorbed in philosophical thoughts and ideas.
- You have few hobbies, but those you do have you explore in depth.
- You communicate best one-on-one or in small groups.
- You tend to become uneasy and irritable when you don't have enough down time.
- You're very selective when it comes to activities and socializing.
- You're territorial – you desire private space and time.

---

[5] *Based upon Hirsh & Kummerow, 1989; Keirsey & Bates, 1984; Lawrence, 1985; Myers & Myers, 1980, as found at http://www.davidsongifted.org/db/Articles_id_10274.aspx.*

- You're quite content to be alone and yet often feel lonely in a crowd.
- You become drained around large groups of people and are uncomfortable going to parties, especially when the host has invited people you don't know.
- You need time alone to recharge.
- To function at your best, you need regular downtime.
- You prefer self-directed activity over group work.
- You are usually cautious when meeting people.
- You're reserved, quiet, and deliberate.
- You don't enjoy being the center of attention.
- You're protective of your private thoughts.
- It is likely you have only a handful of very close friends.
- You may even avoid calling an acquaintance a friend, because you view friendship as something earned over time.
- You hesitate before speaking.
- You reflect back to the person you're speaking with to make sure you're understood –and understanding.

Obviously, nothing is absolute when it comes to introversion, extroversion, or anything else for that matter. Some of the above descriptions will serve you well as a network marketer. Others will have to be negotiated around. Nonetheless, the preceding should be viewed as giving you permission to honor yourself when developing your network marketing business and warn you of the potential pitfalls of certain behaviors. The following chapters should help you negotiate these challenges and use these opportunities for growth to your advantage.

Tools you can use and still remain authentic

In her landmark book, *Quiet: The Power of Introverts In A World That Can't Stop Talking*, Susan Cain identified qualities which Eric Worre and Jim Rohn would recognize as key tools for network marketing success, such as:

- Listening
- Quiet Persistence
- Planning
- Sincerity

Given that you likely have these social skills in abundance, it is possible to tweak them for use in your new profession. The following quote from Cain explains how:

> If you're an introvert find your flow by using your gifts. You have the power of persistence, the tenacity to solve complex problems and the clear sightedness to avoid pitfalls that trip others up. You enjoy relative freedom from the temptations of superficial prizes like money and status. Indeed your biggest challenge is to harness your strengths. You may be so busy trying to appear the zestful, reward sensitive extrovert that you probably undervalue your own talents, or feel underestimated by those around you. But when you are focused on a project you care about, you probably find that your energy is boundless.

So stay true to your own nature. If you do things in a slow and steady way, don't let others make you feel you have to race. If you enjoy depth, don't force yourself to seek breadth. If you prefer single-tasking to multi-tasking, stick to your guns. Being relatively unmoved by rewards gives you incalculable power to go your own way. It's up to you to use that independence to good effect. [6]

Introverts got game

There is evidence why Cain's advice is well placed. Research at the University of Wisconsin by psychologists John Brebner and Chris Cooper tested and proved the theory that, "introverts are geared to inspect and extroverts are geared to respond." [7]

Their research started with a simple game.

1. Participants were asked to press a buzzer every time they saw a "good number."
2. If successful, they won points. If it was a "bad number," they lost points.
3. Through experience, participants began to know which numbers were which.
4. A 50/50 mix of introverts and extroverts took part in this study.
5. But some — the extroverts — kept pressing the "bad" numbers.

[6] Cain, Susan. *Quiet: The Power of Introverts in a World That Can't Stop Talking*, New York: Broadway Books. 2013. 173

[7] Ibid 166

6. Indicating that extroverts are more impulsive than their introverted peers.
7. Introverted participants determined what was going wrong;
8. Then stopped pressing the button when the "bad" numbers appeared.

This difference reflected the fact that extroverts are more motivated by rewards than a well-played game. Consequently, extroverts consistently got lower scores because they moved too fast in a quest to get the most points.

Meanwhile, introverts fared better because they wanted to play the game well. Cain notes, "If you focus on achieving your goals, as reward-sensitive extroverts do, you don't want anything to get in your way — neither naysayers nor the number nine. You speed up in an attempt to knock these roadblocks down.

"Yet this is a crucially important misstep, because the longer you pause to process surprising or negative feedback, the more likely you are to learn from it."[8]

I can attest to this truth, because my sales percentage is above the average of my peers. I learned early on that going too fast made me miss important clues. I slowed down, made sure I communicated well, and only "pressed the button" when I felt confident I would receive a positive response. I have found that if I honor my authentic voice, I don't sell, I educate; I don't convince, I communicate; I endeavor to serve the needs of the customer before my own.

---

[8] Cain, Susan. *Quiet: The Power of Introverts in a World That Can't Stop Talking*, New York: Broadway Books. 2013. 166

Success does not require extroversion

Today's world is filled with successful introverts. Unfortunately, their success is what makes them seem more outgoing than they actually are. Yet the truth is that their success was born of quiet introspection. "When you're socially awkward," poet and philosopher Criss Jami writes, "you're isolated more than usual, and when you're isolated more than usual, your creativity is less compromised by what has already been said and done. All your hope in life starts to depend on your craft, so you try to perfect it. One reason I stay isolated more than the average person is to keep my creativity as fierce as possible. Being the odd one out may have its temporary disadvantages, but more importantly, it has its permanent advantages."

Today's Network Marketing Tip: Introverts are responding to signals from their amygdala when they feel shy and fearful of being out there. Their frontal cortex can help them get past the fear but not eliminate it. So, all you introverted network marketers out there, before you enter a stressful situation, focus your energy for a moment on your frontal cortex. Ask it to calm your amygdala down. Like a three-year-old at an adult birthday party, the amygdala needs a time out to give you a chance to discuss matters in a relaxed manner.

[1]*The amygdala is an almond-shape set of neurons located deep in the brain's medial temporal lobe. Shown to play a key role in the processing of emotions, the amygdala forms part of the limbic system. In humans and other animals, this subcortical brain structure is linked to both fear responses and pleasure. (sciencedaily.com)*

If you recognize yourself in the above description, the time has come to embrace exactly who you are. Use what Gandhi called, "satyagraha," meaning "firmness in the pursuit of truth" in defining your business purpose. Introverts have led nations and political movements throughout history. Obviously Gandhi was a soft-spoken man. Yet this George Washington of India employed restraint in the face of withering hostility and through his deep inner strength changed the course of history. Here's how he described his communication techniques.

> I have naturally formed the habit of restraining my thoughts. A thoughtless word hardly ever escapes my tongue or pen. Experience has taught me that silence is part of the spiritual discipline of a votary of truth. So many people are impatient to talk. All of this talking can hardly be of any benefit to the world. It is wasted time. In reality, my shyness has been my shield and buckler. It has allowed me to grow. It has helped me in my discernment of truth.

Chapter 5. Preparing Your Mind and Heart

"As an introvert, you can be your own best friend or your worst enemy. The good news is we generally like our own company, a quality that extroverts often envy. We find comfort in solitude and know how to soothe ourselves." ~ Laurie Helgoe

I could have started with how to run your business, but introverts will need some assistance getting into the groove. Hence I am going to outline how you can set the stage to help you feel comfortable within the profession.

First, ask yourself some serious questions. Be honest with yourself; your success depends on it. Think about your answers and write down your thoughts. Chances are you will find solutions to some of your concerns as you keep reading.

1. When I am comfortable, how well do I interact with others?
2. How much down time do I really need a week?
3. Can I make and keep my own schedule?
4. How much time can I honestly spend prospecting for new leads?
5. If I had leads that were people I knew or who shared my interests, would I be able to make warm calls as opposed to cold calls?
6. How well do I tolerate the word, "No"?

The truth gives you wings

Second, contrary to what some companies and people will tell you, be aware there is nothing easy about network marketing. It is a process. There is no such thing as getting rich quickly. Prepare yourself for a three-to-five year period of building your team. You'll make money in slow incremental ways at first, but as your team grows, so will your prosperity.

Third, be prepared for a lot of flak. Your friends and family are likely to hassle you with, "Oh, that's a scam." "You'll never make money at that." "I know someone who tried that and all they got was a garage full of stuff they'll never sell." If you have picked your company well, none of these things will be true.

Remember: many companies use this model. My company chose network marketing as a distribution method because our product requires some explaining. Many companies choose this model for that reason. Others choose it because they want to cut the wholesale piece — the middle man — out of the equation, so people get a better deal. Avon, Tupperware, Legal Shield, and Mary Kay are all network marketing companies. Millions of people make a living using this model.

What do I say when friends criticize?

When friends say any of the above, ask them what they mean. Most likely they are referring to the pyramid model as it existed half a century ago. Today's network marketing — also known as Multi-Level Marketing (MLM), Relationship Marketing and Direct Selling — is an entirely different thing. I like to think of it as a tree that grows and branches out as more people join the team. An associate's hard work can absolutely make it possible for that person (branch) to bear more fruit than the person (branch) further up the tree.

Network marketing takes time

The challenge lies in the notion or perception that it is easy, which is why some people sign up and fail. It isn't that the model is flawed. It is that the person believed they would be that rare exception to the rule that building a network marketing business takes time. So you have to prepare yourself to balance steady, consistent effort with acceptance of incremental progress.

As a network marketing associate, you have to be able to muster the faith to move on in spite of ridicule and rejection. In fact, every MLM company expects that level of dogged persistence. Fortunately, introverts are especially adept at going the extra mile. This character trait can be further enhanced by choosing a company with great tools and trainings that provide a blueprint for success.

However, there is one key ingredient only you can give yourself: the courage to work on your dream thread by thread, without the need for exterior validation. Here is where the advice of Darren Hardy comes in handy.

> When people get started in a new endeavor, they almost always overdo it. Of course, I want you to feel excited about setting up a rhythm for success, but you have to find a program you can absolutely, positively do in the long term without renegotiation. I don't want

you thinking about rhythms you can do for this week, month or even the next ninety days; I want you to think about what you can do for the rest of your life. The Compound Effect — the positive results you want to experience in your life — will be the result of smart choices (and actions) repeated consistently over time. You win when you take the right steps day in and day out. But you set yourself up for failure by doing too much too soon.[9]

Hardy is suggesting that you learn how to pace yourself when developing new habits. Remember that it took you 20, 30, or even 40 years to develop the habits that may have cost you some of your dreams. It will take concentration and self-discipline to train yourself to do things a different way. For example, if you want to lose weight, it may be helpful to have a coach, but the motivation still needs to come from within. (More on the role of coaches in Chapter 13.) If you try to lose more weight than you can physically, emotionally or mentally imagine yourself doing, you may succeed in the short term but will most likely fail in the long run. So the idea is to say, "This week I will lose some weight. It doesn't matter how much," rather than, "This week I'm going to lose 25 pounds."

---

[9] Hardy, Darren. 2013 *The Compound Effect*: Boston, MA. Da Capo Press: Boston: MA. 110

The Caterpillar Parable

Now here is something I would like you to digest slowly.

Just as the caterpillar becomes the butterfly, there is that cocoon time. It's the time when you're making a decision to be the most authentic you possible. In that time you are learning how to change, how to let the raw, slimy ooze determine the strength of your wing. You are delicate in this time and must feed your mind a healthy diet of self-awareness.

The same rule applies for the inward network marketer. Change for an introvert must be incremental but consistent. The caterpillar must surrender to the change slowly if it is ever to become its most authentic self. The caterpillar allows the fallow period but keeps the transformation in mind. Every caterpillar has a list:

- Feed yourself a nutritious diet
- Seal the cocoon tight
- Relax
- Let go
- Believe
- Become the alternate version of yourself

This is how the caterpillar becomes the most authentic version of itself.

Applying this lesson

Honestly assess how many friends you can connect with in a week. Look at your natural rhythms. If you average two or three calls to friends a week, start by *consistently* making three contacts a week. As your confidence grows, your natural rhythm will grow to four or more consistent contacts a week and beyond. Your natural rhythms reflect what feels organic to your nature, so it's easy to stay consistent, and staying consistent is as important as persistence in this business.

In the time I have been in network marketing (since August 2013), I have been able to expand my natural rhythm from an average of four or five calls a week to consistently calling five or six people *a day*. I have found that when I am having a rough week, I will call the people I am closest to before I will call people I hardly know. This helps me stay consistent in my efforts. I am careful not to let this become a crutch, but it does help me stay in my rhythm and thus sustain one aspect of my momentum. If I start to rely on friendly voices too much, the other part of my momentum slows. Like a juggler balancing spinning plates, I have to remember that the object of this business is to build broad and deep teams of business builders. If all I do is call the same five close friends over and over, I am defeating my purpose, which is to add plates, and build momentum and excitement. So I reach back to my list and add a plate (or plates) to remain in the mode of consistently building upon my team. The last thing I want is to do is get bored. If I do, all the plates will come crashing to the floor — including those friendly voices that sustain me.

There are times I will mix things up by spinning some extra plates, just to see if I can expand my natural rhythm to include them. That's how I went from four a week on average to five or more a day. But I do it when my personal rhythm says I am ready. I listen to my authentic self.

Self-awareness is vital

To be ready to operate your business, this sort of self-awareness is vital. It is also something that may allow you to make excuses for why you can't do something. Here is where we have to do battle with our habits and embrace improving our skills. We have all overcome things we couldn't do, such as walking, riding a bike, doing a crossword puzzle. The same is true with this kind of career. If you want to be a professional, you have to stop making excuses and trust that you have every single skill (and then some) required for success. Study after study has shown it, as you will soon learn. Make this your mantra every time you attempt to second guess yourself:

> *If I'm ready to help myself the Universe will help me;*
> *If I'm ready to complain, I have to help myself.*

Psychologist Mihalyi Csikszentmihalyi tells us, "A person has to learn to provide rewards to herself" in order to develop the level of autonomy that leads to self-confidence.[10] Self-awareness and trust allow you to stay in this state of flow. (More about flow in Chapter 13.) As such, simple rewards like a productive day are enough to sustain you. In such a state you will feel balanced and able to work for hours without any acknowledgement of your exterior environment. The voices of the naysayers will melt away.

---

[10] Csikszentmihalyi, Mihalyi. *Flow: The Psychology of Optimal Experience*. New York, NY: Harper Perennial Modern Classics. 1990. 16

This state of flow requires making up your mind to be the most resilient person you can imagine. You will have to look toward the three-to-five year success "horizon" in between every call and every meeting. Apply every tool for concentration and quiet persistence you have in your arsenal.

> Train yourself to spend energy on what's truly meaningful to you instead of on activities that look like they'll deliver a quick buzz of money or status or excitement. Teach yourself to pause and reflect when warning signs appear that things aren't working out as you'd hoped. Learn from your mistakes. Seek out counterparts (from spouses to friends to business partners) who can help rein you in and compensate for your blind spots.[11]

It's crucial that you make decisions from a place of strength, not fear. Abundance is relative. Embrace the abundance you have, and be at peace with what it looks like. Let go of fear. Release neediness as an unnecessary anchor on your soul. Most network marketers don't start making money until their one year anniversary. Be okay with that. Don't compare. Work at your own pace. If it takes years to realize your goals, so be it. The important thing is to let yourself be okay with where you are now while also being committed to

---

[11] Cain, Susan. *Quiet: The Power of Introverts in a World That Can't Stop Talking*, New York: Broadway Books. 2013. 170

moving forward. This is the secret to making the next call, and the next after that. It is the glue that holds your presentation together. You will make the choice to be "the best you" in any given moment. It is a choice to allow transformation to happen so you can be your authentic introverted self.

Always learn, always grow!

If you need help, get it. Acknowledge fear. Use your sounding board to release it and turn to your mentor to strategize about it. Your empowerment will prepare you for delayed gratification. This is your life: you must accept 100% responsibility for it. Read, study, and listen to motivational books and CDs. Don't listen to negative people. Do establish your business from a heart of peace (if you don't understand what that is, read *The Anatomy of Peace* by the Arbinger Institute[12]). Seek winning partnerships and help others recognize their gifts. Look for the most natural path to manifest self-discipline and follow it the whole way. Remember, success starts in the mind. Draw from past successes and imagine only greater success in the future.

Having tackled those things, let's look at creating the right environment for your network marketing business.

---

[12] Arbinger Institute. *The Anatomy of Peace*, New York, NY: Penguin Books. 2008

Chapter 6. Preparing to Go Into Business

"If opportunity doesn't knock, build a door."~ Milton Berle

Now that you have your head and heart in the right place, there are a few physical things you will need as you prepare to start your business. Besides the website the company usually provides, you'll need a list of tools, a list of upline contacts, and the number for corporate support within easy reach. I suggest posting the necessary phone numbers on the wall in front of where you will work, so you don't waste time hunting them down all the time. Remember: time wasted is time you're not connecting, and connecting is critical for success.

Today's Network Marketing Tip: Whatever company you choose, find one that has ongoing free training and leaders who are committed to their teams. If you don't have support, you will falter. As Ernesto Sirolli said, "The death of the entrepreneur is solitude." Also, seek leadership willing to put in the work of educating the public about the product, technology, and ethos of the company.

Furthermore, make sure all the websites and blogs you refer to regularly are saved in your browser's Favorites, so you can access them quickly. Don't forget to alphabetize and replace outdated information as soon as new contacts and tools become available.

If you're on a budget, take advantage of whatever brochures and support materials your company provides. If you can afford brochures and fancy business cards, go for it, but remember, it's going to be a while before you're making money, so what you spend today should be easily absorbed in your budget. This also goes for trainings. Be selective. Go to the convention — because that where the really juicy stuff is revealed — and to a regional if the speaker is exceptional, but don't spend money on fancy workshops held at five-star resorts that promise you'll be rich in a week after attending. It is much more likely that your tools will give you exactly what you need to prosper if you use them well. While these things are deductible, that benefit won't help you if you're spending money today for a deduction you won't be able to take advantage of for another year.

> Today's Network Marketing Tip: Create a quiet space to make your calls and demand family (or roommates) respect your need for undisturbed time. According to America's Best Franchises, "If your home is too small and you are crammed in with noisy children, it will indeed make it more difficult for your business to work." Your work space doesn't need to be fancy, but it should allow you privacy, quiet, and dedicated storage space for maximum ease of operation.

The importance of self-care

Next, arrange for self-care. Your emotions are key to your success. There's a saying in network marketing, "If you're feeling down, reach up; if you're feeling up, reach down." I would take this a step further. In addition to reaching down to lift up someone who is struggling, it is important to reach up and be strategic about who you reach up toward. Your upline may not be a good choice. I recommend finding yourself a mentor *and* a sounding board. Usually these are two different people. The mentor should be able to answer questions like, "How do I approach a prospect in this situation?" The sounding board should be okay with you saying, "I feel discouraged and need to feel support." Mentors rarely want to hear your discouragement. They want to help, solve problems, and offer solutions. Having a buddy — maybe you return the favor — who lets you be angry, discouraged and frustrated but then doesn't let you off the phone until you've been able to get back on a positive track, is an amazing benefit that will help you last the three to five years it will take to build your business. Take heart! You can find comfort and education if you're willing to ask for it.

Another step might be making sure you have solid evidence, not just anecdotal evidence. Find a way to offer measurable results to friends, family, and leads. For example, if it is Tupperware, buy two heads of lettuce and put one in a Tupperware container and the other in the usual plastic bag you get from the grocery store. Take a picture of the two containers with a date visible. Store as usual in the fridge for a couple weeks. Take another picture and then post the results side-by-side on a Facebook or Pinterest page (see Chapter 10). By showing it's not just some anecdotal baloney, you'll get a much better response.

Reflect Who You Are!

This next item should be obvious but many people fail at this simple technique for network marketing success. What is it? Be yourself. That's right: simply be yourself. If you try to be high pressure and you're normally a person who is laid back, you'll turn people off. Even if someone doesn't know you, they will sense you're fake, and fake translates into lack of credibility. If you're an introvert like me, you may have to stretch a bit, or come up with creative ways to reach more people and still honor your personality, but you must honor your introversion so you come off as genuine.

Introverts are naturally gifted with constitutions that make them careful, even cautious. Consequently, they usually avoid wasted energy and failure by observing and planning before they act. As you prepare your business, take the time to honor that about yourself. Nonetheless, this is not an invitation to make excuses for not moving forward. Take whatever steps you can, even if they are only incremental steps. This is essential. The calls won't be made by themselves. The events won't happen without you. The sale or recruitment won't happen either. Your participation is vital — and forward momentum is key.

Set goals!

Heed the advice of motivational speaker and sales trainer Brian Tracy. "Top people have very clear goals. They know who they are and what they want. They write it down and they make plans for its accomplishment. Unsuccessful people carry their goals around in their head like marbles rattling around in a can. A goal that is not in writing is merely a fantasy. And everybody has fantasies, but those fantasies are like bullets with no powder in the cartridge. People go through life shooting blanks without written goals — and that's the starting point."[13]

I recommend setting simple, doable goals at first, and then slowly working your way up to more challenging days. Note I said, "more challenging days," not "impossible days." For example, as an introvert starting out in network marketing, you may think a single phone call to a friend is doable, but making 10 calls is impossible. So make your goal that day to make that one phone call. Then challenge yourself. Try making two calls a day, then three, and so on. By the time you've reached 10 calls, you can probably jump ahead to making 15 calls in a day, and then 20. The idea is to get used to how it feels to make a call, like easing into a hot tub. Eventually the whole process will feel like second nature. The same goes with other goals, such as making sure you attend events, working your social media pages, and working a given number of hours. All these goals will create patterns in your mind and rid you of the failure habit. Now each day will be filled with incremental triumphs until you finally are comfortable with success.

---

[13] Hardy, Darren. 2013. *The Compound Effect*. Boston, MA: Da Capo Press: Boston. 71

If your introverted downline associate seems to be spending too much time preparing, be sensitive to why. By knowing why, you will be able to address the issue rather than berating her or him into giving up. Do what you can to help that person gather the appropriate information to make more educated choices to move forward. Remember, while it is true that introverts will keep trying to solve a puzzle long after the extrovert has given up, it is also true that feeling pressure to perform will result in feeling overstimulated and thus increase the likelihood of giving up.

This quote from introverted psychologist and educator Ester Bucholz is worth remembering, "Others inspire us, information feeds us, practice improves our performance, but we need quiet time to figure things out, to emerge with new discoveries, to unearth original answers."[14] Therefore, a balanced approach is called for with your introverted associate. Encourage, support, assist, and praise all the effort the associate is making to move ahead. Be gentle on the subject of cold calling. Offer to be the third voice to help an introverted associate learn the ropes, perhaps even starting with a three-way call to a close friend or family member. Listen and understand her perspective. This will move things along, help you retain team members, and generate success for everyone.

---

[14] Bucholz, Ester. *The Call of Solitude*. New York: Touchstone Press. 1997.

Chapter 7. Communication Matters

> *"Let's clear one thing up: Introverts do not hate*
> *small talk because we dislike people. We hate small*
> *talk because we hate the barrier it creates between*
> *people." ~ Laurie Helgoe*

The good news is: introverts excel in communication.

In *Quiet: The Power of Introverts in a World That Can't Stop Talking,* author Susan Cain cites studies that have shown that highly sensitive people tend to be introverts. Members of this genetic minority are usually "philosophical and spiritual in their orientation, rather than materialistic or hedonistic. They dislike small talk. ... They tend to notice the subtleties others miss--[such as] another person's shift in mood. ... [They] compare choices more closely and think in an unusually complex fashion."[15]

I interpret this to mean that an introverted network marketer is more likely to look deeply at the needs of her or his customer and associates. She is also more likely to wait to

---

[15] Cain, Susan. *Quiet: The Power of Introverts in a World That Can't Stop Talking,* New York: Broadway Books. 2013. P. 136

speak until she has all the facts she needs and, most importantly, will respect that in others. In short, she will listen and observe first and let the rest take care of itself. All of these are qualities she will need in this business.

Speaking of respect, slow down!

This is vital! When you first start out do not call all your friends and say "hey, take a look at my product" or "hey I just joined a network marketing company." You will instantly lose well over half your leads.

Instead, call or text someone and suggest catching up over coffee. Then make it all about catching up. Ask about them first! Listen deeply. Only mention your business if it happens organically and then very, very casually. "Well, as you know I'm out of work, and unemployment doesn't cut it so I'm making some extra dough with an in-home business," or "I'm still at my same job and things are going okay, but I realize I've got to make some more dough if I am ever going to retire so I am also working for this great company with an in home business." If they ask for details you can give them. Otherwise, slow down and just finish the chat like you would with friends.

Remember this is a relationship business and one can blow it if we blurt things out too quickly. This is the voice of experience and I know it has cost me some leads, so I offer it to you as a warning. Introverts have a hard enough time connecting without blowing contacts by making it seem like the only reason you're calling is to make a sale. After all, there's truth in the old saying, "People don't care how much you know until they know how much you care."

Today's Network Marketing Tip: Try it on for size. Many times we are given scripts that sound like someone else. This is like a size XXX trying to fit into a size 6. Everyone is going to know you don't feel comfortable "wearing" the dialogue. Take some time to go through the script and "alter" it to suit your personality. For example, if the script calls for you to use the word "unmitigated," and you are more comfortable with the word "complete," then say, "complete." However, don't make the script a good deal longer than it is. People listen better when the presentation is brief.

Network marketing versus sales

Most introverts cannot even fathom the notion of doing sales as a career. That is why it is important to know the difference between what we traditionally think of as sales and network marketing. For one thing, in traditional sales you make your commission once so you're always at the whim of the customer. For another, you are usually working for someone else and if you have a "bad" month you may get fired. Network marketing means you're your own boss and get commission from customers and associates downline from you. If you have an off month chances are you'll still make some money from another downline associate. Why? Because he has the same amount to gain by working hard that you do. In fact, he may earn more than you do that month. (To learn more, check out: http://www.thebizmodel.com/.)

In addition, the network marketing model is more about educating than convincing. In fact, this is likely true of the best salesperson regardless of which model she employs. "Sales is an outcome, not a goal," notes Jill Konrath, author of *SNAP Selling*.[16] If you educate your customer about why the product or opportunity is wonderful the prospect convinces herself. There is no need for high pressure, "Order today or lose this golden opportunity," kind of salesmanship. All you are doing is educating the person and this starts with good listening skills.

Listen with all your senses

The thing about communication is this: everyone thinks they are good at it. The guy who shuts down every time his wife asks how his day went; the kid who explains why she wants something by screaming for it; and even the woman who shops rather than admit she's lonely. To become good at it, you have to learn how to listen with all your senses. That's right: all your senses!

For instance, you wake up and your partner's made coffee. It's way too strong and tastes like she poured a bucket of grounds into the pot. You ask what's wrong and she says, "Nothing." But in reality she's foregoing her usual careful measurement because she's distracted by something that's troubling her.

---

[16] Konrath, Jill. *SNAP Selling: Speed Up Sales and Win More Business with Today's Frazzled Customers*, New York, NY: Penguin Books: 2010. P. 6

Even your nose can sometimes tell you what a person is saying. If you have ever dated someone who wore too much cologne, you know what I mean. Insecurity has made him communicate the notion that he smells nice and bathes regularly by applying more than just a dab.

Obviously hearing the tone in a person's voice, noticing the directness of a person's gaze, or observing how many times the person touches one thing or another will give you other communication clues. For those who are especially tuned in, your sixth sense may help you judge when to back off even if all other signals are a go.

An essential for successful connections

Steve Shapiro's *Listening for Success* recommends the following technique for people selling a product: "Ask, Listen, Ask, Listen, Ask, Listen…"[17] In short, ask a question then listen carefully to the answer. The answer may not be something as direct as "Yes" or "No." It may not even be as simple as, "Yes, I'm interested, tell me more." A person may be asking a million questions, indicating hesitation, showing interest, getting angry, or trying to think of an excuse to hang up. It can all be in the tone of voice, the look in the eye, or any myriad of other things that indicate an answer to your question. So ask again until you both are clear, and if it looks like it would be a good time to stop, then stop.

---

[17] Shapiro, Steve. 1999. Listening for Success. San Diego, CA: Chica Publications.

When it comes to advanced sales, Shapiro expands upon the "Ask, Listen" model with a four-step process. He points out a distinct difference between just hearing what a person is saying and actually listening. To truly listen, one must:

1. Attend to what a person is saying (offer undivided attention);
2. Acknowledge how they feel;
3. Clarify why a question was asked or a position was taken; and then
4. Respond without necessarily having an answer.

Let's break down each of these steps to understand how anyone — introvert or extrovert — can employ them to the advantage of their network marketing business.

How to be attentive

The greatest gift you can give a family member, friend, or prospect, is to be attentive to what they are saying. This requires what psychologists call "bracketing," the skill of temporarily setting aside any outside distractions or interior monologues. In short, not allowing your own thoughts and impressions to interrupt the other person.

Bracketing lets you make space for the other person's perspective on events and circumstances. For example, while you may have had amazing success with network marketing, your prospect may not have. When he tells you how much he hates it, the common urge is to be defensive and say, "Oh, but my company is different."

Two vital steps have been missed in jumping from hearing to responding. For one, the person will feel you didn't listen. For another, you have limited your access to information that may be crucial to helping that person with his issue. Through bracketing you are able to resist the urge to respond prematurely, thus making the conversation more meaningful for both parties.

> Today's Network Marketing Tip: You don't change a situation by changing the other person; you change a situation by changing a person's response.

How to acknowledge how they feel

The second step sounds easy but is hard to do correctly. For example, you might acknowledge them by saying, "Oh, that's a good point," but then go into something like, "But you don't know anything about my company." When you jump into this sort of defensive posture, you are not employing the two most important steps to their fullest potential.

At this point in the process you may want to say something like, "Oh, that's a good point. You're saying that your failure in network marketing cost you both money and an important friendship." By reflecting back what you heard, you are acknowledging the person's right to their own perspective. Even if you're off the mark about what the person said, you'll display your desire to understand him. This gift will keep the connection between you strong as you move to step three.

> Today's Network Marketing Tip: Adopt an advisory role rather than a persuasive one. People don't buy something because they understand the product but because they feel understood. If people feel that you want to help them personally, they will feel heard and seen in a way that naturally instills confidence.

How to effectively clarify

When you employ step three, you further acknowledge the person by clarifying what you've heard. This allows for both accuracy and deeper understanding between you. You see, if you don't truly understand what a person is saying, it is highly unlikely that you'll respond (step four) to the right message. For example, a prospect says, "You're making all these claims about your product but where's the proof?" You could instantly go to responding by becoming defensive and start offering testimonials and all the studies that have been done. However, by asking a clarifying question like, "Why do you ask?" you may discover the real reason is the person is asking for proof is he's been taken to the cleaners by slick-talking people in the past, and wants to make sure he doesn't make the same mistake twice.

Shapiro notes there are a number of ways one can clarify, depending upon the situation and what your attentive listening is telling you. You can ask open questions like, "What was that like for you? Could you elaborate? Is there anything in particular you'd like to see? How do you mean? Is there anything else?" Or you could make statements like, "Tell me more." The idea is to make sure that you're really responding to the other person's need and not your subjective interpretation of what they are saying.

The difference between responding and reacting

Most people go directly from step one "attending" to step four "responding." This is more like reacting than responding. If you react, the prospect is likely to distrust you. If you respond by specifically addressing the person's concerns (which you've paid attention to, acknowledged and clarified), chances are the person's return response will be much more favorable.

If you discover you don't have an answer to their question, it is always better to say, "I don't know" rather than wing it. Here's where you can use a tool like a three-way call with your upline or a professionally-produced video that explains the product in depth. If you don't know, you can painlessly admit it by suggesting options like those above, or asking another question such as, "Where would you like to go from here?" or "What sort of proof are you looking for?"

The SNAP Method

While Shapiro offers great insights about the listening side of network marketing sales, let's look at the fabulous work of Jill Konrath—how to reach the highly stressed, time crunched prospect. Her method is completely aligned with what Shapiro recommends, as you will see.

Konrath advocates making your product or service explanation: **S**imple, i**N**valuable, **A**ligned and a **P**riority (SNAP). Specifically, the more complexity you eliminate, the more essential you are; the more what you are offering aligns with the prospect's needs and values, the more of a priority it will be to work with you.

"Knowing as much as you can about your targeted prospect is more important than your knowledge of your own product, service, or solution," she advises.[18] This is because people are so hurried and frazzled that if you can't make the product personally relevant to them, they just don't have time for it.

Think of the people you know who are forgetful, easily distracted, demanding, and impatient. Are they people with a lot of time on their hands? Chances are, the answer is no. So if you go into a detailed explanation of the double-blind studies done by your company without even knowing if that matters to the prospect, chances are you will lose her and go into what Konrath calls the "D-Zone," when "sales are Delayed temporarily or Derailed permanently, as customers Default to the status quo. You are Dismissed or Deleted. Your prospects Disappear or they're Dead to you completely."[19]

---

[18] Konrath, Jill. *SNAP Selling: Speed Up Sales and Win More Business with Today's Frazzled Customers*, New York, NY: Penguin Books: 2010. 6

[19] Ibid., 20.

When approached, your prospects are likely asking themselves how much time and effort it will take to hear you out, do they actually trust you know what you're talking about, is this in tune with what they're hoping to accomplish, and whether or not they could just put off a decision to another time.

However, if you employ good listening skills, you will likely forego the canned speech that bores them to tears and has no relevance, and instead pick up on the very thing that will put you in alignment with what they need.

For example, if you sell makeup but have never taken the time to know what skin issues the person has, you will lose the customer. She will stay with her current product because she finally found something that works without irritating her skin. Unless you know exactly what product she already uses and how your products compare, it won't matter how well you've memorized your company's talking points.

When you can't prove you are invaluable and aligned with your prospect, she may dismiss you with, "I'm happy with what I already use," "Oh, that's interesting. I'll get back to you," or "This wouldn't work for me."

Use Shapiro's techniques to learn what's important to her when choosing and using a cosmetic product. Listen carefully and clarify. Will your product work for them? It is better to walk away from prospects than force yourself on them when you realize your product isn't a match. If you spend enough time considering a prospect's needs, you can gracefully back off before losing the connection. By honoring that boundary, you've built trust with the prospect so they may give you a lead to a prospect with fewer skin issues.

Konrath recommends doing a "SNAP Check" before you even approach a prospect.[20] This consists of placing yourself in the customer's shoes before you approach. If you know he has a daily 9 a.m. meeting with department heads, don't call at 8:45 wanting to chat. He won't have time for you even if politeness tells him he to say yes when you ask, "Got a minute?"

If the prospect was disappointed with network marketing in the past, find out the reasons for his unhappiness. If your product is unsafe for children and he has six kids, be prepared with an alternative around it. In others words, your perception, your need to make a sale, and your timeline does not count. Only the customer matters; his needs must be respected above all else.

Konrath's book is chockablock with easily applicable techniques at which you, as an introvert, will excel. You will learn:

- How to use research to get inside a customer's head
- How to understand why your messages were deleted
- What sort of responses trigger you
- How to avoid sales killing missteps
- How to become the prospect's life improvement coach
- How to make it easy to say yes

---

[20] Konrath, Jill. *SNAP Selling: Speed Up Sales and Win More Business with Today's Frazzled Customers*, New York, NY: Penguin Books: 2010. 34

By being the upline someone wants to work with, over the long haul you'll create a more cohesive and sustainable team. Yes, the book is primarily written for the traditional sales professional, but the information will definitely help you build a team large enough and strong enough to keep those residual income checks flowing well into the future.

Introverts and small talk

As noted previously, introverts are much less likely to enjoy small talk. While extroverts use small talk as a means of easing into a friendship, introverts generally do just the opposite — or at least would prefer to.

I love this quote cited by Susan Cain, "When sensitive people are in environments that nurture their authenticity they laugh and chitchat just as much as anyone else."[21]

This has been my experience as well. When I hang out with my friends — most of whom are introverts — we get very talkative, laughing, joking, and swapping stories. But we usually jump right over the, "Isn't this great weather," part of the conversation and launch into, "Is your boss still giving you trouble?" This is because we are sensitive to the things which have made an impact on each other.

On the other hand, I also have introverted friends who grow impatient with my desire to get to the heart of the matter quickly. "Can't we discuss the mundane for a while," a friend once remarked.

---

[21] Cain, Susan. *Quiet: The Power of Introverts in a World That Can't Stop Talking*, New York: Broadway Books. 2013. 136.

Both are stylistic qualities worth recognizing. Sooner or later they will give you clues about how to approach the person.

Because this is our comfort zone — deeper, more meaningful exchanges — introverts sometimes find it hard to step back and allow someone the time to ease into a conversation through the use of small talk. This is a place where we can learn from our extroverted friends. Take a minute to determine the depth a person is willing to go before launching into the level that's comfortable for you. Use your powers of observation and emotional sensitivity to determine when you can go deep. After all, you don't pick up a hitchhiker going 60 miles an hour!

How extroverts can help us

By the same token, our extroverted friends can help us by keeping in mind that interrupting us only exacerbates our reticence. While their enthusiasm to be a part of the discussion may feel natural to them, it leaves us fumbling to retain our thought until we're given the opportunity to finish it. For example, in the excitement of conversation our extroverted friends will sometimes move to an entirely different topic. Now we introverts have to either let go of our thought or find a way to squeeze it in under another category heading. If interrupted too many times we'll just stop trying to engage in the conversation.

Extroverts might even catch us quietly stewing and wonder what is wrong. We'll reply, "Nothing," when in fact we're thinking, "Would you please just shut up and let me finish my thought?" No wonder we're branded as too quiet, sullen, or anti-social. Extroverts can help us in these sort of social situations by giving us a chance to let our personalities shine by exercising compassion for our style.

Inside the cocoon

To help our extroverted friends understand our take on a common conversational moment, allow me to offer a glimpse "inside the cocoon" of introversion by describing the scene as we experience it.

It's a noisy group situation. Everyone is chatting and lively. They all seem to have something to contribute. You wait your turn and finally screw up the courage to make a point but as you start to speak you start to notice how all eyes are on you. You see someone cross their arms. Another person sighs. Another person says, "Go on." You try even harder to find the right words and stumble through some preliminary thoughts. Someone says, "Spit it out." Now you can't even find the original thread of your thought, so rather than look ignorant, you smile and say, "You all make great points." Never mind that you disagreed with almost everyone or found a major hole in their logic. You do not feel safe in that scenario, so you don't speak your truth. There is too much stimulation in the actions and reactions of others.

Sound familiar? If you have been the introvert struggling to find the right words, it certainly will. Perhaps you have been the extrovert waiting for someone to "spit it out."

This challenge of extemporaneous speaking stems from an introvert's aversion to over stimulation. This sensitivity has been proven in a number of studies since the 1960s. As Susan Cain notes:

> Once you understand introversion and extroversion as preferences for certain levels of stimulation, you can begin consciously trying to situate yourself in environments favorable to your own personality — neither overstimulating nor understimulating, neither boring nor anxiety-making. You can organize your life in terms of what personality psychologists call ultimate levels of arousal and what I call 'sweet spots,' and by doing so feel more energetic and alive than before.[22]

Nonetheless, the thing about "sweet spots" is that they can be disturbed by loud friends, driving in traffic, or even a "bad day." Do whatever you can to sustain your "sweet spot" by having the courage to ask for advance notice of speaking engagements, preparing what you are going to say ahead of time, and asking for the quiet space you need to work productively and recharge your batteries.

In social situations, ask your extroverted friend to be your "wing man" in case you're caught in an effort to find the right words. With his compassion and your preparation you will be far more at ease.

---

[22] Cain, Susan. *Quiet: The Power of Introverts in a World That Can't Stop Talking*, New York: Broadway Books. 2013. 124-125.

Whenever possible, give yourself time to prepare. This is especially valuable to introverts. If you know who is going to be there and what the topic of conversation is likely to be, you're more likely to be comfortable in a social situation. This is because you can anticipate what will come up. It follows then, that if you know what you are going to say, chances are you'll stumble less when asked a question. If you're selling a product you don't understand, take the time to understand it as much as you can. If it is something extremely complex, at the very least you should know the company's talking points by heart, then make them relevant to the prospect.

And, by the way, there is no shame in admitting you need help and letting the person with an easier conversational style take the lead.

The importance of follow-up

There are some skills you, as an introverted network marketer, may not be aware of or use to their maximum effect. For example, if you've made a connection with someone, be sure to follow up. Not calling a second, third, or even fourth time, is like dropping money on the ground and not picking it up. And don't worry, introverts! If you've made a connection — and have permission to call the person — it won't matter how many times you call. However, it is a good idea to make your message relevant and unique each time you dial. It once took me eight calls to finally reach someone who called me back because he admired my persistence.

Chapter 8. Making a List, Checking It Twice

"You can make more friends in two months by becoming interested in other people than you can in two years by trying to get other people interested in you." ~ Dale Carnegie

After attending my first convention, I was disappointed by what was offered as training in network marketing. It was more of the same: "Call all your friends from high school." "Talk to people you see buying vegetables at the grocery store." "Tell everyone at work about the product." "Never eat lunch alone." I knew few of these methods would work for me. They just went so far past my comfort zone and the reality of my life that all I would be is a tongue-tied, pushy mess.

Tricks to increase your comfort zone

While you don't want to neglect what has worked for generations of network marketers, there are some tricks you can use to increase your comfort zone. For example, think about the people you know. Who has a "servant's heart"? Now think about whom you'd like to work with. Would you choose someone who is just concerned about herself, or someone who is concerned about others? By choosing the latter, the person who cares about others, you will have a partner willing to go the extra mile. This person would be a real business partner, not a constant drain on your energy. It's no fun working with an "opera singer" who only says, "Me-me-me-meeee!" The right partners help you build your business. The wrong ones slow you down.

Today's Network Marketing Tip: Take a trip down Memory Lane and bring to mind folks who are adventurous, fun, smart, and hardworking. Write their names down, how you know them, and everything you know about them. For example, where they are from, where they grew up, what they do for a living, schools attended and majors, etc. Then imagine how they would respond if they heard from you. Is it likely they will remember something you did together? Then you can try finding them via LinkedIn, Google, etc. and contact them with a hearty, "Hey, I was thinking about that time we went to the conference together and started singing in the elevator. It cracked me up and got me curious. What are you up to these days?" This is a painless way to reopen dialogue with someone who might be a great team member.

Ask yourself, "What product or service is related to my product?" "Who does business with people who would do business with me?" For example, if you represent a health, athletic, and anti-aging product, any industry related to those fields would be a natural fit. Medical professionals in all disciplines, including eyeglass lens manufacturers or distributors, hearing aid companies, and alternative practitioners would be perfect. Who else can you name?

Today's Network Marketing Tip: Find out who your top producers are targeting and follow their lead. It doesn't take an extrovert to reach the type of people who are already interested in working with your product, people your extroverted uplines have already found success with. For example, if they are targeting hairdressers, it would be easy to mention the product to your hairdresser next time you're in for a trim.

Follow the Leader

Now that you have some ideas, start writing down the names of anyone and everyone you know who would fit in those categories. If you can't come up with anyone learn to ask for and give introductions, rather than just getting or giving a referral. This will go a long way toward helping you build a list. When I worked in rural economic development, Dr. Ernesto Sirolli suggested that every member of my board introduce me to 10 people. Within a very short amount of time, I had connections in every field related to my job. You can do the same thing by either asking your upline to recommend some businesses to check out, or by asking friends to introduce you to their provider next time they go in for a visit. For example, a friend says, "I'm going in to see my eye doctor next week." You can say, "Would you be willing to introduce me to her?" Chances are by tagging along and making this connection, the doctor will view you as a potential business partner — if for no other reason than might come in to get your eyes checked at some point in the future. It warms the lead enormously. But be careful not to embarrass your pal by launching into a pitch. Just accept an introduction.

Join, Start, Attend, Tag Along

Although at times the task may seem daunting, there is always a way to reach out. Who do you know who has mentioned a need you can fill with your product? What political or social group can you join — and *enjoy* — that will connect you with a broader circle of people? Consider what your friends and loved ones have in common. Lots of artists? Lots of blue collar? Faith? Music? Then think of how you could find more similar people, your tribe as it were. Faith? Talk to more people at your church, mosque or synagogue, and perhaps even visit a different one in your town to create a broader circle of like-minded folks. Music? Go to as many concerts as you can afford, join choirs, and play in bands to find more folks who love the music you do. The point here is to be among people who feel familiar so you will be at ease with them. It is what some people might call, "networking on purpose."

Another awesome way to build your list through socializing is to join a Successful Thinkers group. The Successful Thinkers Network is a 100% free organization whose mission is to create groups of people who "know, like and trust" each other. If there isn't a group in your town, start one by becoming a Lead Ambassador and getting some friends to work with you on starting it. The training is free and super easy. Go to www.successfulthinkersnetwork.com to learn more.

If you plant a garden and harvest the fruit but neglect to collect the seeds and replant, your momentum is wasted. Do it now! Ask your leads for leads. If they don't have leads, collect whatever seeds will work and plant them.

See Chapters 10-11 for tips on how to use Social Media for connecting with more people.

Chapter 9. Going From Wallflower to Social Butterfly

"Wise men, when in doubt whether to speak or to keep quiet,
give themselves the benefit of the doubt, and remain silent."
~ Napoleon Hill

Now I know coming out of your cocoon and becoming a social butterfly is probably the hardest thing for you to imagine, but if done in a way that honors who you are, it isn't as hard as it seems. The key phrase here is honoring who you are. Don't try to love football if you hate it. Do enjoy opera with folks, if you love it. There is no need for isolation just because you're an introvert. There are ways to enjoy being out and about without sacrificing your comfort zone or trustworthiness.

Only the most misanthropic among us eschews socializing. What it will take is finding your tribe among the millions of folks out there and enjoying their company in the way that's most natural to you.

I have found that Meetup.com is a great place to find like-minded folks. I go to groups that enjoy the same things I do. If someone asks me what I do, I tell them, "I represent a company that is revolutionizing health care." This gets their attention. In time an opportunity will present itself to tell them about my product. This is why it may take a while to build your business. You don't just go to an event and vomit your story all over people. You go, socialize, and then present your product in a quiet but confident way as you would to any new friend.

Today's Network Marketing Tip: This should be obvious but many people fail at this simple technique. What is it? Be yourself. That's right: simply be yourself. If you try to be high pressure and you're normally a person who is laid back, you'll turn people off. Even if someone doesn't know you, they will sense you're fake and when you're fake you lack credibility. If you're an introvert, you may have to stretch a bit, or come up with creative ways to reach more people and still honor your personality, but you must honor your introversion so you come off as genuine.

Some simple conversational techniques

For example, as the group talks about the things going on in their lives, you hear someone say, "Yeah, my family is dealing with [something related to your product]." You nod and listen attentively. You genuinely sense your product may be a good fit for the situation. "If I knew of something completely different that would help, would you be interested in learning about it?" If the person says, "Sure," you have your opening. If a person says, "We've tried everything. Nothing will work," you know you have to approach them slightly differently. An appropriate response at that point would be simply, "Sorry to hear that. Just out of curiosity, what have you tried?" This employs Steve Shapiro's question technique, which allows them to feel secure in revealing their frustration and sense of loss. It also allows you to align with their needs as Jill Konrath recommends in *SNAP Selling*. In time—and you will know it when it comes, if ever—you may want to suggest they try your product.

If you're feeling adventurous, consider starting a Meetup of your own. If you do so with the primary goal of expanding your network of contacts, there will not be a messy sense you're manipulating people in order to make sales. Create groups you would willingly join regardless of whether or not you were a network marketer. That's why I picked groups that made it easy for me to feel at ease and at my best. I started a writer's group, a club for spiritual folks who enjoy socializing, and a group for people interested in UFOs. I have plans for three more groups for people who love singing classic American standards, hearing live jazz and blues, and poets. Already people in my Meetup groups have purchased products from me and some are even considering joining as associates. They did so because I genuinely offered an empathetic ear and a loving heart to address their needs, not because I pushed my product or agenda.

Making events work for you

It is also important to choose your venues carefully. No matter what product you represent, you have to be smart about choosing your location. This is especially important to introverted network marketers. Why make it harder on yourself? If you already have trouble speaking with strangers, why make it more difficult to connect with people? For example, it is unlikely that a bunch of guys at an Ironworkers Convention would be interested in your Avon booth. However, if you're selling tools, ironworkers might be a perfect fit.

> Today's Network Marketing Tip: Enter into a Free Trait Agreement. What's that? It's an agreement you make with yourself to do something out of character for the advancement of your business. If you're an introvert, that thing might be agreeing to go to one networking mixer a week, have at least one meaningful chat, and follow up with that person the very next day. Over time you can renegotiate your "Free Trait Agreement" to make that two, then three mixers a week. This will help you feel less guilty when you turn down the invitations of your more extroverted colleagues.

If you feel comfortable hosting an in-home party for your closest friends and family, by all means do so. Make it a real party to celebrate the launching of your business. Ask guests to bring something so there's a reason for them to attend. There are two reasons why having a launch party is important. One, it gets the discomfort of telling friends you're doing this out of the way early and almost painlessly. For another, it may produce some early customers to commence your business quickly.

You may also want to talk to three close friends who support you but don't necessarily have the same circle of friends. For example, choose a work friend, a sporting event friend, fellow choir member, a member of your church, or someone from other circles in your life. Tell them they don't have to buy anything. All you would like each of them to do is host a party. Promise to keep it a social event only and help him or her out by supplying the appetizers and beverages. Her job is to make sure you're introduced to all the guests. The party can be for as many folks or as few as you feel comfortable with. I find four to six people is a great number for me. I can follow conversations and not get bogged down in trying to remember who is who.

Then *do not sell*, just tell. If someone asks what you do (which is likely), share something that's been helpful to you about your product. "I work for a company that has this awesome technology that's reversing the signs of aging in my face." That's all you'll need to say. Make it informative and fun. You'll be surprised how much you will glean from the experience of listening in a social setting and letting go of the need to sign someone up that instant. If you work it right, you will have a bunch of new friends who find you are a compassionate and interesting person. Because your co-hosts and the guests know you are sincerely interested in them regardless of whether or not they purchase product, they will feel comfortable telling other folks who want or need what you have.

Volunteer!

You might also want to volunteer for a group you support. Whether it is a political group or social cause, demonstrating your desire to help others is a fabulous way to build credibility. In addition to participating in everyday activities, you can help plan events or be a greeter. Just like when you attend Successful Thinkers or Meetup groups, other volunteers will eventually ask what you do and you can say, "I'm a teller at a bank, but I also have this great little part-time thing going that's helping me save up for retirement."

Dutch courage versus learned competence

By the way, since we're discussing socializing, be wary of "Dutch courage." You may think of a glass of wine as "extrovert elixir," but studies have shown the relaxing effect of alcohol can be a double-edged sword. Sure, it might make it easier to loosen up and meet people, but if you aren't able to get relaxed without alcohol, you will soon be an alcoholic. Alcoholics are quick to lose credibility, fry their brains, and be viewed as unreliable. It will be very hard to be a success in anything if people view you in this light.

You may want to take a Dale Carnegie course or join Toastmasters to train yourself to speak with greater confidence. Remember: "many introverts can learn to appear to be extraverted for those times when the need arises."[23]

---

[23] Burris, Jill and Kaenzig, Lisa. *Virginia Association for the Gifted Newsletter.* 1999, Fall. 21.

Today's Network Marketing Tip: Start a Meetup account and have meetings with like-minded folks. Interested in books? Start a book club. Interested in bird watching? Start or join a bird watching group. Sooner or later people will ask you what you do. You can explain that you're a network marketing professional. Within a few short months you'll be busy doing fun things that are also helpful for your business.

According to Drs. Jill Burris and Lisa Kaenzig, "This training should be a part of the educational program for all gifted introverts as it provides them with a useful mask to put on when necessary. Such training comes through instruction and practice in public speaking, debate, drama, music, social skills, dance, and mentoring."[24]

Remember: you're in good company

Introverts sometimes have a hard time getting their message out to the world, but without their voices where would we be as a society? Introvert Eleanor Roosevelt brought the struggles of the jobless and minorities in society to her

---

[24] Burris, Jill and Kaenzig, Lisa. *Virginia Association for the Gifted Newsletter.* 1999, Fall. 21.

extroverted husband's attention and helped the U.S. recover from the Great Depression. Rosa Parks, an introvert, got on a bus in Montgomery, Alabama, and changed race relations in this country forever. Al Gore, who in spite of appearances tests as an introvert, once remarked, "Most people in politics draw energy from backslapping and shaking hands and all that. I draw energy from discussing ideas." He realized the only way to alert humanity to the effects of global warming was to speak out as a politician, a move that was probably scary for his introverted self but a necessary step that just might save the world. In short, introverts can be agents for positive change.

Yes, even you!

Chapter 10. Doable Dozen for Network Marketing Success

"Faith is taking the first step even when you can't see the whole staircase." ~ Rev. Dr. Martin Luther King, Jr.

There is something to be said for explaining things in a step-by-step way. Here's a quick overview of what it takes anyone — introvert or extrovert — to achieve success in relationship marketing.

1) **Have a Passionate Belief in Your Product** – Prospects can tell if you sincerely believe something or if you're just aping a sales pitch you've been taught.

2) **Have a Deep Desire to Help Others** – If your passion for helping others blends with what you are selling, you'll master the art of educating people about the product.

3) **Give and Take** – There's always going to be some give and take. If you want to build your team or gain a customer, you need to give something in return. Whether it is an opportunity for greater financial freedom, assistance with being a good network marketer, or even just a quality product, whatever you give must be of greater value than what you expect to make. For example, if your primary goal is to gain a new team member but you cannot honestly offer someone assistance with their new business, you will quickly lose the very thing you hoped to gain.

4) **Keep It Simple** – Speak in simple terms unless asked for something more in depth. People live busy lives; the more you complicate matters the harder it will be for prospects to follow through. The easier it is to understand, the more likely your prospect will say yes. Inexperienced network marketers try to explain too many of their product's benefits. This is a potential pitfall for introverts who like to use facts when discussing their product. By telling too much, they raise areas of concern that would never have occurred to the customer. Resist the urge to explain everything—and your closing percentage will increase. Remember, let the prospect sell herself by asking questions, not giving answers.

5) **Be Straightforward, Humble, and Likeable –** Honesty is the best policy. Clarity is an incredible tool. People like people who are sincere, humble, and clear with what they are presenting.

6) **Ask Questions –** People love talking about themselves. The only way to find out what someone wants, needs or desires is to ask. Search for ways to ask questions that will reflect her requirements. If she keeps saying 'yes' to your questions, you will know you can meet her needs. In this way she sells herself on the product instead of the other way around. For example, if she says, "I wish my skin looked better." You ask, "What have you tried?" She responds, "Tea tree oil, coconut oil, coffee grounds, cucumber, aloe vera masks, even some expensive brands; you name it I've tried it." You inquire, "Have you tried my company's product?" The answer is, "No." You continue, "Would you be impressed if I told you a famous lab in Germany gave it a five-star rating?" The person says, "Yes! Do you know where I can get it?"

7) **Don't Argue, Make It Relevant** – There's a trite but true saying: The customer is always right even if he's wrong. Even if your potential customer has said something completely ridiculous, it is not your job to convince, but only to gather enough information to align with their personal needs and thus guide them to more relevant knowledge. You may have to bite your tongue or move to a different topic you can agree on. Only by keeping it light can you keep a prospect in play.

8) **Don't Get Angry** – The fastest way to lose the deal is to lose your cool. Never take objections personally. By remaining friendly, calm and pleasant, you will build a reputation of being easy to work with. People will recommend you because most folks prefer to work with people who are easy going.

9) **Feel Free to Name Drop** – If you can honestly use the name of someone who endorses your product, do. Never claim an association where there is none. If you're talking with a friend who knows someone you signed up, be sure to mention that association so you can borrow on the mutual friend's credibility. This helps the prospect feel she'll be in good company if she joins up, too.

10) **Ask for Help** – It may be hard sometimes, but we all have to admit when we're stuck. Ask your colleagues, friends, and family for help when you hit a roadblock. Whether it's a personal or professional matter, getting help when you need it is essential for a healthy personal and professional life.

11) **Don't Bad Mouth Your Competitors** – Never speak ill of competitors. Obviously, you can point out where your product has strengths, and in doing so imply why your product is superior, but there is never any need to directly say a competitor's product is inferior to yours.

12) **Be Fearless** – Ease into the conversation and avoid letting the prospect see you sweat. Even if you're anxious to close a deal, do everything in your power not to show it. Breathe deeply and evenly. Keep a relaxed and confident pace. Remember: employ quiet persistence and take nothing personally. Just keep moving and you'll always get a second chance.

These 12 doable reminders lead to one extremely important point: every contact you make should reflect a desire to make it a win-win-*win* result. What do I mean by adding the extra win? Not only should you and the other person walk away feeling happy, but your connection should also be a winner as the future develops. That's the only viable outcome for long-term success. For example, you and your prospect arrive at a decision. You win because he has decided to join your team. He wins because he has decided to work with you and your awesome company. The future wins because both of you act from a place of mutual trust and understanding that brings more people into your team.

Chapter 11. Using Social Media

"Social media sparked a revelation that we, the people, have a voice, and through the democratization of content and ideas we can once again unite around common passions, inspire movements, and ignite change." ~ *Brian Solis*

Introverts can't afford to neglect social media. In fact, this venue was made for us. It allows us to discuss things we're passionate about from a distance. Social media is a great way to let friends know why you're excited about your business. However, if you don't keep content fresh, people stop coming back. Make a habit of updating your social media daily or at least weekly.

I have accounts with LinkedIn, Facebook, Meetup, Pinterest, Twitter, and YouTube. Here's how I use each of them:

LinkedIn: I connect with the people I know from various past jobs, old friends, and people in the same industries as those I have been in, as well as people with common interests. LinkedIn also allows you to create interest groups. I have joined some for network marketers, one for people looking for work, and still another for health and wellness workers. The one for those seeking work is where I tell folks it really is helpful to one's emotional stamina when job hunting to have a small amount coming in from a network marketing business. This is money above and beyond unemployment — and is especially helpful if their unemployment insurance has run out — because it gives them a sense of being useful to the world. A word of caution, however. A lot of LinkedIn groups do not allow overt network marketing pitches, so be discreet and gentle. Trust that people will find you if what you have to say is interesting enough.

Facebook: I have three Facebook pages. The first is my personal page where my friends can keep track of me. When I have a network marketing victory, I post it there as general information. I do not use this Facebook page as a marketing tool, but it keeps my long-standing friends and family current with my successes and creates "top of mind awareness" of my product.

It is also possible to have a "Facebook Party," inviting friends to be on the page at a specific time and date so you can share ideas and news just as if you were at a real, physical party. This is helpful when friends live far away. While the "party" should be for social and not selling purposes, it can remind people of what you're doing and help them know you're doing well. This alone might make them curious. I have an old I have an old friend who has paid more attention to my attention to my Facebook posts since I started network marketing than she ever did before! I haven't given up and don't grouse about it, so now she's wondering if there's something she's missing.

> Today's Network Marketing Tip: Learn to use social media by acquainting yourself with the lingo and the technology. Follow the rules and protocols, and you can make your business stand out. Zoom, Skype, and other services help you see each other face-to-face, have meetings and do presentations. The meetings can be for strangers or your team. This is especially helpful if some members of your team are far away.

My second Facebook page is my business page. There is no question what this page is for. It is designed to educate people about the product I represent, what I am doing, and encourage them to follow my lead. My rank advancements, my favorite stories, latest science, videos, links, testimonials, and even news about upcoming events are all here. This page is slowly working as a lead generation vehicle and it helps my downlines know what I am doing to build my business.

Next on Facebook is my Network Marketing for Introverts page, which is like a mini-version of this book. Monday through Friday I post a daily tip that a networker can use. My hope is that people with other companies will find it and get so excited about what I'm sharing that they'll want to join up with me. I have friends and associates who check this page out to learn what they can about the business. Thanks to this page, my introverted friends feel it might be possible to bring in a bit of extra dough every month — and who couldn't use extra cash?

Meetup: I already mentioned this in Chapter 9, but here's a recap. Go to Meetup.com. Look for events happening in your area that interest you. Two things are worth noting. One: because this is a people business and it is likely you have a small circle of friends, joining groups may be one of the few ways you get enough leads to make a success of this career. Therefore join, but go because you want to go and because the group reflects your authentic self, not simply as an excuse to increase your numbers. People will figure out you're only there to make money. When this happens they won't trust you, and trust is essential in this business. Two: Do not think of these groups as solely a means to an end. Think of them the way you would if you moved to a new town and wanted to find a place to socialize, practice your faith, or play a round of golf. In addition, the closer the events are to where you live, the more likely you'll attend. Nearby events make it harder to have an excuse to flake out (something introverts are notorious for because we get so uncomfortable with groups). Start attending events regularly. You'll meet a bunch of like-minded people that will be easy to talk to because you already have so much in common.

You may also want to create your own events. I must confess I have found this is somewhat easier for me than groups started by someone else. I feel more in control. I can have the event when I want to, control the number of people who attend, and where we meet. I have also found that over time people in my groups begin to suggest locations and times that I am perfectly comfortable with. The bonds created are genuine and sincere because I started from a place of wanting to *know* more people, not because I wanted to *sell* to more people. The groups I have started have even had meetings without me, which is okay because I am not married to controlling the group. I participate when and where I want to. If the group wants to see a movie I have already seen, I can back out with no loss of face or regret. We have all gotten to know each other and feel comfortable whether I am there or not—but I am still viewed as an important member of the group.

Pinterest: This is a fun way to explore what's really important to you, then share those ideas and things with others. It is primarily a visual social medium. You select images—either from their catalog of posts, the posts of others, or your own—and you post them with some remark about what they mean to you. My Pinterest page is called, "Jenifer's Treasure Map." On this page I have quotes from great writers I admire, bits and pieces about my product, motivational quotes, photos I have taken, and small pieces of poetry about them, pictures of houses I like and design elements for a future date when I can have those things. It helps to visualize in order to materialize. I find it a great motivator. As friends and family look to see what's on it, they become subliminally a part of my network marketing world.

Twitter: The trick here is learning how to be short but sweet –or should I say, "short but tweet"? You're limited to 140 characters — that's characters not words, so you have to remember to say LOL instead of Laugh Out Loud (3 characters instead of 14). While this may seem obvious, the literate introvert may be tempted to use multisyllabic words or phrases. You can open an account for free and search for phrases like, "I lost my job," and find people who are seeking income, or a phrase that reflects what your product offers. Respond to results with many followers, so it doesn't look like you're targeting an individual. This is called trolling and is frowned upon. Make a point to retweet things that seem exciting or interesting to you, especially if they reflect your product area and personal interests. This will draw people to look at your profile. If your links are too long and eat up too many characters, try bitly.com which helps shorten links. Personally, Twitter is my least favorite social media.

YouTube: This social media site is cracking down on network marketers so you have to exercise caution and not just make extended commercials. Content must reflect another interest unrelated to your product and not refer people to your sales page. That being said, creating a YouTube Channel is easy and fun. Either you can post your own videos — which I recommend if you feel comfortable doing so — or you can post those of others. There's space for blogging and comments about the videos. The videos should be under 14 minutes but may be longer with permission. You must have the copyright to those videos if over 14 minutes, and videos you share from others must be given an acknowledgement. For example, I might put a friend's video about mountain biking up and say, "Video courtesy of Randy Dreiling." Then I can talk about how my product improves stamina and the various professional cyclists who are using it as part of their training regimen. Or I can film myself giving a testimonial, or talking about my week. The important thing is — as much as your skill will allow — make these home videos more than just talking heads. Generate before and after videos of yourself. You can film events. Tell a story with pictures and music. As long as these are short — ideally between three and five minutes — you'll get plenty of hits when someone goes to YouTube and types in key words related to your product. This makes people anxious to see your site and learn what's new.

Social media requires some consistency and discipline to stay on top of it. See Chapter 14 for tips on how to make social media a part of your regular work day.

Chapter 12. Use Your Tools

"It's best to have your tools with you. If you don't, you're apt to find something you didn't expect and get discouraged." ~ Stephen King

When you first start out in network marketing, you'll feel like a fish out of water. So much about the model is unfamiliar. That's when it is important to utilize whatever tools are out there, even if that tool is a more extroverted upline or downline! How can you take what your upline is teaching and use it in a way that feels right? Sometimes all it takes is a little creativity and courage to get to the next level.

Today's Network Marketing Tip: Remember that this is relationship marketing. You don't have to work alone. Your upline should be there to help you along. Ask for leads, ask for three-way calls, ask for encouragement, and don't be shy about needing help. If your team is in this for the mutual benefit of everyone, then every direction should be a two-way street.

Use your upline as a resource

Your upline is likely to be much more familiar with the ropes or at least the company. She will be able to tell you what documents you'll need, what books to read, how to keep track of sales, manage your website, etc.

She is also handy for three-way calling. In case you're unfamiliar, this tool — the three-way call — is essential when you need another voice to lend credibility, back you up, fill in knowledge gaps and, believe it or not, impress your prospect with how well connected you are.

In a recent training, an associate explained that, when he schedules a callback, he tells the person, "I'll call you back to make sure I have some expert answers for you." This is his way of opening the door to a three-way call. When he calls the person back he says, "This is So-n-so, a Diamond with my company. Since she knows so much more than I do, I figured it would be great to bring her in on our call to make sure your questions are answered accurately." This helps the prospect feel cared for and may help you close the sale faster.

A well-run company knows that it takes a village to build a successful team. Accordingly, it encourages communication across all layers of the organization. The beauty of such a network marketing company is when your immediate upline is not available there is likely another upline willing to help out as well.

For example, say you have a prospect who insists on talking to someone about the science of your product. Your upline is a liberal arts major and doesn't understand it any better than you do. You can arrange to have an upline with a science background answer the person's particular question and in the process learn something yourself. Or perhaps you or your prospect don't understand the pay structure. You've looked at all the videos and watched all the trainings but you're still confused. Someone else in the binary structure could probably explain it better than you can. By using this person as a resource to explain the necessary steps for mirroring his success, you are much more likely to successfully recruit your prospect.

Get to know your tools

Tools are the bones of your business. All the brochures in the world are useless if you don't have other tools to leverage them. In addition to helpful team members, a good company will have terrific associate support and a great back office for your website, as well as all kinds of webinars, videos, testimonials, and training tools for you to use personally and professionally.

Organize your tools

It bears repeating that the first thing you should do when starting your business is acquaint yourself with your tools and keep a list of testimonials, brochures, websites or other items handy for whatever situation may arise.

I find that it helps to have tools organized by topic or use. For example, if you're selling a health supplement, have a list of the various science explanation tools handy, as well as a list of upline contacts (including their time zone), a list of relevant brochures by category (athletic, business, brochures in

Spanish, etc.), and a list of books to refer people to, among other things. The idea is to make it as easy to access the information quickly without letting a prospect "cool" while you search for the right document or link.

Just as you select a flat or Phillips head screwdriver based on the task at hand, it is important to choose tools that are appropriate for the job. There are tools for skeptics and tools for the curious — and they are not necessarily the same. When speaking with someone, suss out what sort of person they are before offering a tool. I have had prospects who weren't influenced by videos and links, but were completely inspired by testimonials. I had others who could care less about anecdotal evidence and only wanted hard scientific data.

Part of the "ask, listen" mantra mentioned in Chapter 7 is finding out what sort of thing will motivate the person to try the product or take on a distributorship. The more questions you ask the closer you will be to finding the right tool. So rather than just dump a bunch of tools on a person, spend some time figuring out what the right one will be. This will help you help your prospect, and make closing easier and faster.

Maintain your greatest asset: you!

There are even tools for you. Reading the right books to stay on track will work wonders on your staying power. Steer clear of things that destroy your motivation, such as pessimistic and negative articles or books denigrating your product. Watch videos two, three, even four times to make sure you understand them. Listen to motivational CDs in your car on the way to a presentation or, for that matter, whenever you drive. This will give you the fire you'll need to face a group. Friends that support you can also be an awesome tool. They will give you space to be frustrated but not let you give up. A friend once said, "Don't worry about failing because you're not gonna quit!" While it didn't instantly make my fear go away, it did give me a mantra to say to myself and thus another tool I could use in developing my business.

A clear mind is the greatest tool of all. This means giving yourself time to process information, rest, relax, and recover. I spend at least 30 minutes a day in meditation. It helps me relax and feel spiritually refreshed. As often as possible I spend a while walking or exercising. Then I spend 15 minutes planning what I am going to do in a day, including which calls I am going to make, what things I need to prepare, and where I need to go. A few minutes of planning helps the brain feel less anxious when meeting strangers or making a follow-up call. You'll know what to say and how to say it. You'll have the right tools ready to share. Clearing the mind helps you avoid using a sledge hammer to drive a penny nail.

Chapter 13. Supporting Your Introverted Downlines

"Only those who care about you can hear you when you're quiet." ~ *Author Unknown*

Let's start this chapter with a humorous reminder from Jonathan Rausch: "Someone you know, respect, and interact with every day is an introvert, and you are probably driving this person nuts."

Your connection with your introverted business partners should start with accepting them as they are. This helps build their business while stabilizing your own. To preserve the sense of acceptance, it is important to be less like a boss and more like a partner.

Consequently, I will reiterate some things expressed elsewhere in this booklet just in case you either didn't catch them the first time or skipped over them because—as an extrovert—you wanted to cut to the chase!

Chances are you already have an introverted friend. You know the type: the person who goes to work and then comes home to enjoy his favorite hobby rather than go to a party; the renowned presenter who speaks to thousands but doesn't sign autographs; the cousin who chats away happily when the two of you are sitting on the porch after Thanksgiving dinner but who clams up entirely when the entire clan is sitting around the table; or the associate (someone like me) who attends the convention and maybe even a team event but has to retreat to her room afterwards to recharge her batteries.

These are just some examples of introverted individuals. Introverts might be shy, depressed or insecure, but they aren't all that way. They might look like the nerds you teased in high school or former Vice President Al Gore. In other words, not all stereotypes apply when thinking of introverts, but there are some hard and fast truths about how they relate to the world:

1. Introversion is neither a pathological or abnormal condition.
2. Introverts comprise between 35-50% of the total population (most modern studies lean toward the latter figure).
3. Introverts may represent a minority of the population but are a majority in the gifted population (Gallagher, 1990; Hoehn & Birely, 1988).
4. Introverts get their energy internally and find social interaction draining. Extroverts are just the opposite: they get their energy from being with others and are drained by being alone.
5. The introvert's main focus is the internal world of ideas and concepts (the mind); the extrovert is primarily concerned with the external world of people and activities (Myers & Myers, 1980). It is also important to note that introverts usually live inside their inner worlds and rarely let others into

them, which may lead you to make erroneous decisions about them and their needs. For example, if an introvert is quiet, it doesn't necessarily mean she's sad or angry. She just may be processing something.

6. Because extroverts often do not understand the introverted mode of being, they think it is their job to try to help the introvert become more social, verbal, and outgoing. This generally has the opposite effect. When pushed, introverts become even more drained, taciturn, and withdrawn.

7. In a scholarly article for the magazine *Education*, Dr. Arnold Henjum places introverts into two distinct categories:

   a) **Group A** [the one often mistakenly thought of as extroverted, e.g. this would be someone like the author of this book]: Self-sufficient, confident, hardworking, with firm goals, self-actualizing, reserved, preferring activities that involve inner experience and introspection; and

   b) **Group B:** Shy, timid, withdrawn with low self-concept, lacking in communication skills, demonstrating fear of people, dread of doing things in front of others, preference for being left alone. [Note: It is possible some of the qualities mentioned in Group B are the consequence of frequent criticism for not being more social or more outgoing.] [25]

---

[25] *Education*, 2001, Vol. 101:1:39

How to relate to your introverted downline

When it comes to the "care and feeding" of your introvert, it may be helpful to remember that introverts usually prefer to find solutions themselves. While your intention is to be supportive by providing a possible solution, it may shut an introvert down to say, "I felt that way myself and this is what I did." To an introvert this may communicate, "Your fear isn't valid."

While obviously the point of this booklet is to help introverts get past their fears, it is also true that a fear must be acknowledged before it can be conquered. So automatically saying, "This is what I did to get past my fear," ignores the fact that you, as an extrovert, may be suggesting something an introvert cannot bring herself to do.

For example, the introvert says, "I am afraid I don't have enough people on my list." The extrovert replies, "I had that fear myself, so I went to a bulletin board and pulled off all the business cards and started calling those people." This is sure to produce a "deer in the headlights" look on an introvert's face.

Instead the extrovert's first rejoinder might be, "Tell me more about the fear. Where does it start?" This opens the introvert up and helps her feel safe. She explains. You hear that she has called all the people she can think of. Instead of asking her to do something as overly stimulating as cold call everyone on a bulletin board, you might ask something like, "Have you looked at Eric Worre's memory jogger? There's a lot of great ideas there."

This allows the introvert to feel she can use her research and study skills to find names she hadn't considered. It supports the introvert in a way that is in sync with her personality and allows her to build her marketing muscles gradually. Remember: one cannot run until one first walks. By slowly building her muscles with lukewarm leads, eventually her fear will dwindle to a manageable size.

You can also help your introverted downline get started by understanding her "why," and making sure she has the right tools from the start. By doing this, you will make her first steps simpler and more rewarding. You may also offer to do a three-way call with someone she already knows, such as a close friend or family member, so it doesn't feel as threatening the first time out the gate.

> Today's Network Marketing Tip: Don't be afraid to release your inner introvert. While introverts may need encouragement to relate on a more superficial plane, their extroverted colleagues should be grateful for an introvert's ability to make it safe to be serious.

Listening encourages better than soothing words

In *Listening for Success*, Steve Shapiro makes this wise observation about how he felt when his father said, "You'll do fine." Shapiro writes, "Have you ever known someone to say, 'Wow! Thanks! I guess I don't need to worry anymore because you said I'll be fine.'?"

Shapiro was looking for someone to simply listen as he expressed feeling apprehensive. While his father intended to soothe Shapiro's fears, the remark actually shut him down. People, regardless of whether they are introverts or extroverts, don't like to have their fears dismissed or solutions offered unless specifically asked for. They would rather be heard.

How to build a sustainable team

It is interesting to note the observations of psychiatrist and philosopher Carl Jung: "Extroverts have a high rate of fertility, lower powers of defense and shorter duration of life [while] introverts are equipped with numerous means of self-preservation plus a low fertility rate." While fertility may be the result of the number of an extrovert's sexual conquests and not actual physiology, the fact remains that careful introverts have fewer accidents and more consistent results.

We see this most visibly in the animal kingdom, where species with high sensitivity tend to breed and grow in population (e.g. deer and rabbits), while the more aggressive or outgoing species (such as tigers and wolves) are often the most endangered. The same can be true of humans in network marketing teams. Too many "bold animals" put the team at risk. Through careful cultivation of "sensitive animals," the team will incrementally grow.

The website introvertspring.com notes that introverts respond to extroverted pushiness by either going into their shells like "turtles" or becoming "prickly porcupines." Either way, the result may be to drop out of the team if the upline doesn't respect the associate's needs.

Like turtles, introverts arm themselves with a protective outer shell. This comes in handy when we face people and situations that endanger both our energy levels and self-esteem. It also helps us survive insults and criticism from insensitive extroverts. Unkind words bounce off our shells instead of penetrating our soft, squishy interior. Our shell manifests itself in our guarded nature. We tend to be slow to trust new people and slower still to reveal our true selves to them.

For some introverts, metaphorical armour isn't enough. Years of enduring hurtful comments from brash extroverts (i.e. "you're weird," "party pooper," "you're too quiet") can cause us to develop a porcupine-like exterior. Often, neither sword nor shield can protect us from hurtful words and situations. Instead, we internalize things. We begin to believe that something is wrong with us. We become like a wounded turtle whose shell has been ruptured.

Even if you mean well, saying things like, "You're too quiet," only states the obvious and has the unwanted side effect of making an introvert shut down or withdraw even further. In fact, it may even make the introvert force herself to be outgoing with disastrous results. If she doesn't have time to think through her responses, she may come on like a freight train in an effort to be extrovert-like. I know this is true for me. I used to have a friend who badgered me all the time about being quiet, so when socializing with her, I would force myself to talk about anything and everything that came into my head. The result? Sounding crazy. I'll never forget overhearing a third party say to her, "*This* is your quiet, brilliant friend Jenifer?" By allowing your introvert to be herself, you will protect your relationship and your team.

The introvert's inner child

While it is unlikely you'll see kids selling network marketing "lemonade" at a roadside stand any time soon, it is true that the inner child of an introverted associate must be nurtured with sensitivity. Bear in mind, most introverts had a rough time in school. Branded as nerds, stand-offish, quiet, not a team player, arrogant and even perhaps snobbish, introverts often feel isolated and misunderstood. Consequently, when supporting an introverted colleague, it is wise to take her inner child into consideration. In the book *Quiet*, author Susan Cain suggests the following techniques for helping an introverted child feel safer socially — methods I believe are also relevant to adults.

> One of the best things you can do for an introverted child is to work with him on his reaction to novelty. Remember that introverts react not only to new people, but also to new places and events. So don't mistake your child's caution in new situations for an inability to relate to others. He's recoiling from novelty or overstimulation, not from human contact. … The key is to expose your child to new situations and people — taking care to respect his limits, even when they seem extreme. This produces more confident kids than either overprotection or pushing too hard.[26]

---

[26] Cain, Susan. *Quiet: The Power of Introverts in a World That Can't Stop Talking*, New York: Broadway Books. 2013. 248

How the hare can adjust to the tortoise's pace

By keeping lines of communication open, you will discover what pace is best for your team member, and know when and how it is appropriate to encourage forward momentum. If you're consistently supportive in helping your associate navigate social situations, you'll see a remarkable shift in behavior. Eventually she will learn how to regulate fearfulness and be able to reassure herself. "Oh, I get it. I can do what those extroverts are doing, maybe not exactly the same way, but I can be safe meeting new people."

One way to help an introvert learn to be okay in social situations is to be among the first people at an event. This helps your colleague avoid the potentially stressful activity of breaking into an existing party full of people. He will feel like other people are joining him in a space he's already familiar with, rather than asking him to break into a group already deep into socializing.

How to reward an introvert

When it comes to rewarding your introverted team members, let me warn you that the usual rewards often fall flat. Researchers studying the "reward system" of the brain have discovered that extroverts have a larger dopamine delivery system than introverts, which may account for the introvert's aversion to spontaneity, and preference for predictable results.

As psychologist Daniel Nettle notes, "Introverts have a smaller response [to rewards] and so go less out of their way to follow up reward cues."[27] This may explain why it is often the extroverts who get excited about prizes and giveaways, while introverts have only mild enthusiasm for the chase. The latter are less likely to stray past their comfort zones to get a prize. Nettle's research backs up the Brebner and Cooper study found in Chapter 4 that indicated introverts may be better at playing a game but are not motivated by winning.[28] It may make sense to determine what turns your introverted team member on, and privately offer a similar reward for a goal met. This doesn't mean there shouldn't be team-wide rewards, but it is much more likely for an introvert to respond to a personal goal than a team goal.

> Today's Network Marketing Tip: Encourage members of your team to arrive at conventions and other corporate events a day or two early to meet, before being thrown into the hubbub of the larger affair. This allows the introvert to have several touchstones he is already familiar with. This way he won't feel so alone amidst the crowd. Associates can compare notes, locate missing team members, and even share in each other's success.

[27] Cain, Susan. *Quiet: The Power of Introverts in a World That Can't Stop Talking*, New York: Broadway Books. 2013. 161

[28] Ibid. 166-167

Introverts and large events

Large events filled with crowds of extroverts can make an introvert want to crawl into her shell. I love the observation of Criss Jami, "Asking an introvert to go to a party is like asking a saint to go to hell." This certainly is true for me, particularly if I don't know anybody, or it's likely to get loud and rowdy.

When I first started with my company, my upline insisted I attend a convention a month later. While everyone else was engaging in small talk and "rah-rah-rah," I felt out of place and overwhelmed. I was looking for something deeper, something I could care about. As the crowds swelled in an orgy of cheerleading, I could feel the life being sucked out of me. To make matters worse, she insisted I attend every social event she went to, when all I really wanted to do was decompress and recharge my batteries. On top of that I was dealing with excruciating, throbbing back pain, thanks to the venue's incredibly uncomfortable metal folding chairs.

Not only did I have to disguise my sense of being overwhelmed, I had to attempt to mask how much pain I was in. Instead of being pleasant and charming, which I am perfectly capable of being given the right amount of "battery life," I was grumpy and quiet. I knew I wasn't making a great impression but I did not have the energy or reserves to make the best of it. I felt ignored, unseen, and unheard. I was told I'd "get over it" and that I just needed to "get out of [my] own way."

"You have to be coachable," one extroverted executive told me. When I asked what she meant, she said, "You have to learn to be friendlier. You don't strike me as very interested in people. Just get out of your own way and stop being quiet." If I didn't like my upline as much as I do, I would have walked out right then and there.

In social situations like these, the introvert will try to lean on the two or three people he knows. However, the extroverts could get so swept up by all the energy in the room that they leave the introvert feeling even more isolated. Author Jonathan Rausch correctly observed, "For introverts, to be alone with our thoughts is as restorative as sleeping, as nourishing as eating."

Thus when everyone heads to dinner, the introvert finds himself hoping for a seat at the end of the table so he can beat a hasty retreat to re-energize. When people ask how he feels about the event, he feels obligated to say he's enjoying himself, because he knows if he doesn't he will be viewed as someone who is not a team player. With all the celebrating he has little time to think and even less to create. He begins to sigh and complain. He drinks too much "extrovert elixir" in an effort to fit in. Eventually he expresses his desire to leave the event early and is often faced with the disapproval of his peers for not joining in the fun.

Why introverts get overwhelmed

The fact is, conventions and other events are generally no fun for the introvert. It is overstimulation on steroids. While it is unreasonable to ask team members to chill out and discuss something of depth, there are a few things extroverts can do to make such events less onerous.

First, get to know your introvert's limits ahead of time. Encourage him to stretch those limits as much as possible. Plan to get there early so your introvert can navigate the social situation from a place of relative strength. Make things easier by introducing him to as many people as possible beforehand.

For another, give him a task that will occupy him during a large event. If he serves coffee or issues name badges, he'll have a task that allows him to stay focused on one person at a time. There is also something to be said for the control this gives the introvert. It helps him feel stronger when he has something important to do.

Finally, give your introvert an exit code word ahead of time. This is his signal that he's reached his limit, and calls for you to defend his decision to leave early. For example, the agreed upon signal could be when the introvert says, "My, I'm beat." That's your cue to say, "If you need to go rest up before the big day tomorrow, go ahead. I'll bring you up to speed with what happens here over breakfast." This signals your support for the associate and discourages the rest of the group from insisting he stay longer. If they do, it's your job to make sure the introvert is backed up in his decision to leave early.

You might suggest your introverted downline take a Dale Carnegie course or join Toastmasters. This will have a two-sided benefit. Not only will he learn to be more at ease in social and speaking situations, but he might also find incredible leads in a more natural way.

What does "coachable" mean?

Incidentally, here's my take on the whole "coachable" thing. When an upline says, "not coachable," what is really being conveyed? "You're stubborn, inflexible, and not like the rest of the team." If one views the job of coach as being a skilled teacher capable of reaching individual team members —something all good coaches do—then it is more likely an introvert will learn what she needs to, because introverts are more studious than extroverts.

If an upline is a "go out there and win one for the Gipper" kind of coach, with a "just do it" whether you have that talent or not attitude, the type who is more interested in the game than the individual, he will lose the introverted downline. Sure, that might be fine if the "coach" is okay with losing 35-50% of his players. But if he wants to build a wide and deep team that will stand the test of time, keep him at the top ranks, and have a sizable number of "players" who long to play the game well, then the coach needs to learn the right way to reach and teach those who are wired differently.

Summary

To summarize, here are six key factors to keep in mind when working with introverts:

1. Don't think of introversion as something that can be fixed. Think of it as a different style of social interaction. While at times people act like extroverts, don't assume it's easy for them. Remember the two styles of introvert mentioned on page 91. That surface impression masks intense discomfort and emotional stress. It doesn't mean they can be

extroverted if they want to. The best you can hope for is that they will enter into a personal "Free Trait Agreement" allowing them to play the role as often as they feel comfortable doing so (*see Chapter 9 Tip*).

2. Balance your training methods to make sure introverts feel comfortable and understand what is expected of them. Introverts prefer independence and need plenty of downtime to absorb what they've learned.

3. Introverts can become very focused on one or two aspects of the business. Encourage them and help them find like-minded colleagues.

4. As much as possible, do collaborative work in smaller groups, so introverts feel comfortable speaking up and are not overshadowed by the extroverts in the room. Introverts work well in pairs, as they support each other in social activities and help one another find the right words.

5. Avoid throwing an introvert into high intensity social situations when they just start out. They are likely to bolt, clam up, or feel discouraged that they'll never fit in.

6. Remember that extroverts like to have attention called to themselves. They thrive on that acknowledgement. Introverts get their energy from within, so may actually feel uncomfortable if asked

to stand up in front of a group to accept an award. Praise and reward your introverted downline privately so she can absorb the accolades quietly and in her own way.

What's in it for you?

You may think, "Yeah, yeah, why should I tiptoe around my introvert?"

Well, here's my answer. It will help you build a more sustainable and successful team.

Studies have shown that introverted leaders are 20 percent more likely to follow suggestions and 24 percent more likely to build teams with better results.[29] When downlines are empowered to take initiative, their teams outperform those led by extroverts by 14 percent. [30] Teams view introverted leaders as more approachable and receptive to ideas, which motivates the team to work harder.

Because of their inclination to listen to others and lack of interest in dominating social situations, introverts are more likely to hear and implement suggestions. Having benefited from the talents of their followers, they are likely to motivate them to be even more proactive. ...Employees who take advantage of opportunities in a fast-moving, 24/7 business

---

[29] Cain, Susan. *Quiet: The Power of Introverts in a World That Can't Stop Talking*, New York: Broadway Books. 2013. 57

[30] Ibid. 56

environment without waiting for a leader to tell them what to do, are increasingly vital to organizational success. To understand how to maximize these employee's contributions is an important tool for all leaders. It's also important for companies to groom listeners as well as talkers for leadership roles.[31]

Introverts have the persistence, listening skills, and self-reliance any busy leader would want on her side. They'll stabilize your team, be aware of challenges ahead of time, and work with less ego and more team spirit. In short, introverts are worth the effort of adjusting to their personality style.

[31] Cain, Susan. *Quiet: The Power of Introverts in a World That Can't Stop Talking*, New York: Broadway Books. 2013. 57-58

Chapter 14. Nurturing Your Future

"You are the architect of your own destiny; you are the master of your own fate; you are behind the steering wheel of your life. There are no limitations to what you can do, have, or be, except the limitations you place on yourself by your own thinking." ~ Brian Tracy

If you're going to keep going in this business, you have to develop "quiet persistence." For most introverts, this is relatively natural. Instead of giving up when faced with a difficult prospect or day, focus your attention on the horizon—your goal—and just keep plugging. You may have to climb over a few rocks on your journey, but if you make a habit of being quietly persistent you will reach the horizon and beyond. Quiet persistence is not being a pest. That's noisy pestilence. Quiet persistence is being willing to move forward past the obstacles without whining and crying about them. Onward!

You'll also want to catch yourself every time you make excuses for why you can't get something done. Consider why something else is a higher priority. It's important to distinguish between what's vital and what's not. For example, if you feel you need to spend more time with your family

because you have been neglecting them, it's ⌐
so. Down the road that neglect will take more ⌐
than making room for daily connection now. On ⌐
hand, if your goal is to make a living with your busi⌐
you've been spending six hours a day with your kids bu⌐
two on your business, things might be out of balance.
Negotiate an appropriate amount of time with household and
familial tasks, then get to work. The same goes for those who
do networking marketing as a means to make a second
income. Don't neglect your job in favor of your business or
you won't have that stable income most people need to start a
network marketing business. And while you're working on
your business, be sure to spend more time making calls and
generating leads than arranging the files on your desktop.
Otherwise you'll have no business to neglect!

Today's Network Marketing Tip: There are two kinds of
people: those who trust and those who don't. Those who
do will likely take a look at your product. Those who
don't will need a compelling reason to do so. Start slow
with every prospect. Discern which category he or she
belongs to and if that person is the untrusting sort,
determine where the hot buttons are. Then research a
compelling reason to look at your product. It can be a
personal, professional, or spiritual reason. Arrive at the
right question to ask and/or information to give from a
place of compassion. Then listen and wait. You'll hear
the sound of trust being built.

riorities and keep track of your progress

Darren Hardy, author of *The Compound Effect*, cites the importance of setting daily priorities and then assessing how well you met these goals at the end of the day.

> Every morning I have what I call my calibration appointment...where I take fifteen minutes to calibrate my day. This is where I brush over my top three one-year and five-year goals, my key quarterly objectives, and my top goal for the week or month. Then, for the most important part of the calibration appointment, I review (or set) my top three MVPs (Most Important Priorities) for that day, asking myself, 'If I only did three things today, what are the actions that will produce the greatest results in moving me closer to my big goals?' Then, and only then, do I open my email and send out a flurry of tasks and delegations to get the rest of my team started on their day. I then quickly close down my email and get to work on my MVPs.[32]

Clearly Hardy knows what an energy vacuum email and social media can be, so he limits that activity to a given time of day. If you don't, you are far more likely to spend time on activities that draw you away

---

[32] Hardy, Darren. 2013 *The Compound Effect*: Boston, MA. Da Capo Press: Boston: MA. 103-104

from your top goals. On the other hand, if your goals include keeping your social media activities current, then spend as much time as you need on things related to your business, but forego the cute videos of puppies your Facebook friends are sharing.

Today's Network Marketing Tip: You may have lost your tough boss in favor of being your own boss, but make no mistake: you have to be a tough boss of yourself to succeed in this business. Push yourself to make those calls, attend those meetings, listen to testimonials, and accept constructive advice. Work it like a business. Manage yourself and your downlines with compassionate motivation.

At the end of the day, perform what Hardy calls "cashing out." This is making sure that everything you did that day matched the MVPs you set for yourself that morning. You do this by balancing the actions you actually took (Accounts Payable) with what you set as your priorities (Accounts Receivable). If they do not balance, determine why, and work to remedy whatever distraction kept you from meeting your priorities. Don't beat yourself up; just take notice.

For example, one of your priorities for that day may have been to attend a Kiwanis Club luncheon. Instead you found yourself designing a flyer for an event three months from now which wasn't a priority. Now think about why you did that instead. Was it because you didn't feel like facing a bunch of strangers or being social? Was it because drawing is more fun?

Whatever the reason, face it head on and ask yourself, "Why am I scared of strangers?" "What would it take for me to feel more social?" "Is there another time I can devote to my love of drawing so I don't risk my business by avoiding what is a greater priority?" Once you have the answers to these questions, you will be able to direct your energy toward your priorities.

These steps might look something like this:

Question: "Why am I scared of strangers?"
Answer: "I am scared of strangers because I feel threatened when I don't know people."
Question: "Why would a bunch of Kiwanis members hurt me?"
Answer: "No reason."

So next time there's a Kiwanis meeting, make that your priority. Tell yourself, "I'm safe with Kiwanis Club members," and then go. By asking questions of yourself until you feel safe, you can stay on task and make balancing your accounts easier.

Today's Network Marketing Tip: Follow-through with your prospects, customers, business associates, and team members, is essential to building a sustainable and growing business.

Take care of your garden so your harvest is great

Allow your garden of leads to grow organically by weeding out the time wasters and doing all you can to plant your seeds in fertile ground. If you sow where you are most comfortable tilling, with seeds for the types of plants you enjoy most, your harvest will be great. If you try to reach too far beyond your comfort zone — or plant in ground that's not your own — you'll likely spill a lot of seed that will never take root.

A good way to reinforce your momentum is to remember this is *relationship* marketing. Send thank you cards when people purchase your product or join your team. Send gifts when people reach certain milestones. Honor friends of friends as if they were friends. Treat prospects as if they are already a part of your team. Put on your "big boy" pants and treat people respectfully regardless of their relationship with you.

This goes back to what I said about communication and list building (Chapters 7-8). Those who listen carefully will prosper more quickly than those who ignore the needs of those with whom they are speaking. If you ignore their needs, you're ignoring the relationship piece of relationship marketing. People who feel heard and seen are much more likely to refer friends and family to you. Those who reflect that respect by following up with prospects as promised, will find themselves with a fortune in good will.

Bear in mind that your customers also contribute to your team. Their success with your product will bring other people into your business as either additional customers or associates. I regularly call people who have purchased my product and ask how it is working for them. It doesn't have to be a super long call. It can be a simple, "Hey, I was thinking of you and wondered if you're noticing any improvements and if you had any questions?" Then I might ask how much they are taking, when they take it, and what their results have been. This tells me if they are using the product correctly to have the results I hope they will. If I fail in this step, a person may use the product incorrectly and thus not get results, leading to a greater probability they will drop out.

"Checking in" greatly improves the likelihood they will continue as preferred, autoship customers, enhancing the stability of my commissions. In time the relationship will feel strong enough that I may be able to ask if they would like to become distributors themselves.

The same applies for people after they have become my business associates. I make sure I follow up every now and then, first being certain they have the tools they need and are introduced to as many members of the team as possible. I encourage and support them so they feel like part of the team. As their upline, I view it as my duty to make sure they feel comfortable with the process, regardless of whether they are introverts or not.

Manage your relationships

Network marketing means you never have to work alone. Just as you should be there for your downlines, your upline should be there to help you along. Ask for leads, ask for three-way calls, ask for encouragement, and don't be shy about asking for space to recharge your batteries. If your team is in this for mutual benefit, every relationship in every direction should be a two-way street. Honor those relationships as you would a valued friendship. After all, even those members of your team who sometimes rub you the wrong way are contributing to your success.

Yet it is also important to remember that you get in life what you tolerate. Tolerate inefficiency and things grow more inefficient. Tolerate people who make excuses and you get more excuses. Tolerate negativity and you get more negatives, and it just keeps compounding, day after day, year after year, until you have nothing but zeroes in your life. You wouldn't bank somewhere if their interest rate compounded in reverse, reducing your investment instead of growing it, would you? In short, there are times when some people are more trouble than they are worth. Their negativity can destroy your flow.

"Creating a positive environment to support your success means clearing out all the clutter in your life," Darren Hardy notes in *The Compound Effect*. "Not just the physical clutter, but also the psychic clutter of whatever around you isn't working. Every incomplete promise, commitment, and agreement saps your strength because it blocks your momentum and inhibits your ability to move forward."[33]

---

[33] Hardy, Darren. 2013 *The Compound Effect*: Boston, MA. Da Capo Press: Boston: MA. 138.

Plan ahead!

Introverts are great planners. We know how to get the most out of opportunities. Keep an eye out for places to reach your target market where you'll feel comfortable. For example, I recently saw an article in the paper about an annual women's conference at the Senior Center in a nearby community. I arranged to have a booth at the event. Rather than force myself to meet the 200 women who were there, something I would be very uncomfortable with, I put together an attractive gift basket and had an entry form in each bag. Then it was just a matter of going to the tables as women sat down, showing them the form, and suggesting they fill it out for a chance to win the prize. Out of 200 women, 74 women turned in the form, providing my team with leads we didn't have before. Naturally, after hitting 24 tables, I had to retreat for a few moments to recharge my batteries, but those previous few minutes of discomfort were well worth it. I spoke with some great people and had some solid warm leads by the end of the day.

The following chart shows how I divide up my day. Obviously those hours are very flexible. Sometimes I spend four hours on calls and zero on business-related tasks. Other times I devote all day to an event. I have found that a schedule helps me keep track of my business and stay motivated. I try to do at least some of each every day. This is just a sample I made using Excel. Your version may be a Day-Timer or a similar planner that keeps you organized and focused.

TASK	Mon	Tue	Wed	Thur	Fri	Weekend
Business Tasks (filing, email, books)	9-10	9-10	9-10	9-10	9-10	
Phone Calls to Leads	10-10:30	10-10:30	10-10:30	10-10:30	10-10:30	
Who?						
Follow-Up Schedule (with whom, when?)						
Follow-Up Call Made (who)						
Contact existing partners/customers	10:30-11	10:30-11	10:30-11	10:30-11	10:30-11	
Who? How?						
Build New Leads	11:00-12	11:00-12	11:00-12	11:00-12	11:00-12	
What Was Done?						
Clubs	1 hour		1 hour		1 hour	
Which One						
Events	2 hours		2 hours		2 hours	
Which One						
Motivational Study		1 hour		1 hour		
What was done?						
Social Media	1 Hour	1 hour		1 hour		
Which Ones						
Charge Up/Vision Call	1 hour	1 hour	1 hour	1 hour	1 hour	
What I Learned/Anecdote						

Maintain your momentum

Make your work days count. Consistency is the mother of a prosperous business. If you only work your business sporadically, you may never build a successful business. Even if you can only work your business three hours a day, make those hours a regular habit. Don't let anything interrupt the pattern. The universe rewards steady, concentrated effort.

Why is this so important? Because psychologists and sociologists have performed studies that have proven there is such a thing as a "flow." It happens when one pursues an activity for its own sake, not for the rewards it brings. In this state, things happen more effortlessly. Those who study this phenomenon have noticed that fulfillment comes from putting energy into an activity that is truly meaningful instead of activities that bring a quick buzz, excitement, or even distraction. In a "flow," one can work for hours without distraction and remain persistent, even consistent, without worrying about outcome.

If you find yourself beginning to move out of your flow, redirect your activity to something meaningful. For a network marketer, especially an introvert, one must be vigilant against things that tell you they have meaning but don't, like organizing your pencils and pens by color. If it is meaningful, it will move you toward your goals, without being about the reward of achieving them. For example, consistently making calls and building your list is meaningful and keeps you in the flow. Doing the same with the idea that you'll make a sale every third call takes you out of the flow.

Too often, people get their business rolling but fail to do whatever is necessary to keep it going. This is like putting only a gallon of gas in your car for a cross-country journey. You need to fill completely and refill as necessary to make it the whole way. Strange as it may sound, eventually you will build enough momentum that you will go farther faster. There is no way to over-emphasize the importance of building and sustaining momentum. Without consistent, sustained effort, your business will flounder. Resist the urge to rest on your laurels.

Ask yourself, "If I would get fired for not making five calls today, would I be willing to make them?" Weigh the benefits of staying focused against the instant gratification of your bad habits. Give yourself an "atta girl" (or "atta boy") and keep going no matter how far up the ranks you rise. Even at the top when it is possible to take a breather, don't rest too long or your engine will be cold and your momentum will be stopped.

As long as we're discussing consistent effort, let me make it clear that I do not mean boring effort. Switch things around, stretch your legs, do something you never tried before, all in the service of keeping momentum going. Getting bored can be just as much of a momentum killer as stopping all together.

Here's the hardest step you may have to take to sustain momentum: fire your upline. Not literally, of course, but mentally. If you find your upline has lost passion, makes excuses, shows up late to meetings, or is not available when you need her, the time has come to let her go before her struggles become yours.

The truth is, momentum can be destroyed by all kinds of things. Boredom, fear of success, jealousy, frustration, reaching a goal, even certain people can stop your business in its tracks. Make a commitment to stay in the flow so your momentum is continuous.

Always be a student

One of the most important things you can do to nurture your business is to always be a student. For most introverts, this goes without saying. In fact, learning something new is our favorite part of the day. Read inspirational works, how-to books, motivational works, and even something just for fun. Study your product's field to be on top of the latest research, and quote it as part of your confidence-producing educational talks. All of these things will help you stay motivated and lead to network marketing success.

On the other hand, one of the best pieces of advice I ever got was from a retired Amway rep. He said, "You will be approached by every Tom, Dick and Sheila, to attend motivational workshops, business building seminars, and network marketing success trainings. Some are good but they'll drive you broke. They'll say, 'Now that we've taken you to this level you'll want to learn the *real* secrets by buying this level.' Sure, these classes are deductible and some may even teach you stuff and get you pumped. But it is better to invest in CDs and books and establish a great relationship with your team. That's a far better use of your resources."

> Today's Network Marketing Tip: Learn to trust yourself. If you trust yourself, people will naturally trust you. They will sense a quiet confidence in you. They will look to you for assurance and truth. By honoring who you are and living an ethical, compassionate life, your world will be surrounded by people who love and admire you. They'll tell their friends, "You have to meet my friend. She walks her talk." There is no greater accolade than that.

You can beat the odds!

Finally, don't let yourself become a statistic. You can beat the odds as discussed in Chapter 3 by planning well, following through, removing roadblocks, and setting goals that sustain your momentum. While at times the task may seem daunting, one can turn that around by deciding here and now to drive yourself forward, regardless of how hard it may seem at times.

Give yourself a reward for each statistic you beat. Let the reward graduate with the difficulty. Make note of your anniversary. Celebrate it as you would a birthday or wedding anniversary. Make it past the first year, and take yourself and your team out for dinner. Make it past five years and treat the whole crew to convention tickets. Reach year ten and celebrate with a trip to Bermuda or some other place you'd enjoy.

By the way, make this last trip all about you. You will have earned it!

Chapter 15. Great Reads to Help You in the Process

Adler, Jordan	Beach Money
Anastasi, Mark	The Laptop Millionaire
Ancowitz, Nancy	Self-promotion for Introverts
Arbinger Institute	The Anatomy of Peace
Blanchard, Ken	Lead With Luv (with Colleen Barrett)
Bristol, Claude	TNT: The Power Within You
Brown, Brene	The Gifts of Imperfection
Bucholtz, Ester	The Call of Solitude
Cain, Susan	Quiet: The Power of Introverts in a World That Can't Stop Talking
Carnegie, Dale	How to Win Friends and Influence People
Covey, Stephen	7 Habits of Highly Effective Network Marketing Professionals
Covey, Stephen	7 Habits of Highly Effective People
Elsberg, Sandy	Bread Winner, Bread Baker
Fenton, Richard	Go for No
Hardy, Darren	The Compound Effect
Helgoe, Laurie	Introvert Power: Why Your Inner Life is Your Hidden Strength
Hensley, Dennis	The Power of Positive Productivity
Hill, Napoleon	Think and Grow Rich
Kiyosaki, Robert	The Cash Flow Quadrant
Maltz, Maxwell	Psycho-cybernetics
Maltz, Maxwell	Zero Resistance Selling
Maxwell, John C.	Put Your Dream to the Test: 10 Questions to Help You See It & Seize It
Olson, Jeff	The Slight Edge

Pritchard, Paula	Owning Yourself
Rohn, Jim	Building Your Business
Rohn, Jim	The Five Major Pieces to the Life Puzzle
Rohn, Jim	12 Pillars (with Chris Widener)
Sandberg, Sheryl	Lean In
Sirolli, Ernesto	Ripples From the Zambezi
Shapiro, Steve	Listening for Success
Solis, Brian	Engage: The Complete Guide for Brands and Businesses to Build, Cultivate and Measure Success in the New Web
Tracy, Brian	The Miracle of Self-Discipline: The No Excuses Way of Getting Things Done
Tracy, Brian	Change Your Mind, Change Your Life
Ury, William	Getting To Yes
Worre, Eric	Go Pro: 7 Steps to Becoming a Network Marketing Professional
Zach, Devora	Networking for People Who Hate Networking
Ziglar, Zig	See You At the Top!

Acknowledgements

My sincerest thanks go out to Tami and Chuck Gates for their support and encouragement, Nancy Peyron and Deborah Maher for the kick in the pants, and my team, both up and down lines, for their efforts in helping me build my business. I would also like to thank Rachel Wolf for editing this work. Lastly, I would like to thank Susan Taylor for her wisdom, guidance and love.

Made in the USA
Lexington, KY
12 May 2015